DATE DUE

OCT 21 '99			
DEC 2 '00			
NOV 7 02			
GAYLORD			PRINTED IN U.S.A.

How
Honesty Testing
Works

How Honesty Testing Works

John B. Miner
and Michael H. Capps

Q

QUORUM BOOKS
Westport, Connecticut • London

Library of Congress Cataloging-in-Publication Data

Miner, John B.
    How honesty testing works / John B. Miner and Michael H. Capps.
      p.   cm.
    Includes bibliographical references and indexes.
    ISBN 0–89930–980–1 (alk. paper)
    1. Employment tests. 2. Honesty—Testing. 3. Truthfulness and
falsehood—Testing. 4. Lie detectors and detection. I. Capps,
Michael H. II. Title.
HF5549.5.E5M54   1996
658.3'1125—dc20   96–15352

British Library Cataloguing in Publication Data is available.

Library of Congress Catalog Card Number: 96–15352
ISBN: 0–89930–980–1

First published in 1996

Quorum Books, 88 Post Road West, Westport, CT 06881
An imprint of Greenwood Publishing Group, Inc.

Printed in the United States of America

The paper used in this book complies with the
Permanent Paper Standard issued by the National
Information Standards Organization (Z39.48–1984).

10 9 8 7 6 5 4 3 2 1

Contents

Acknowledgments

There are many people who have contributed to this book, either knowingly or unknowingly. Since the book draws heavily on research dealing with honesty testing, we are inevitably indebted to those who did that research. This has not been an easy field in which to work and what has been accomplished, given the obstacles, is rather amazing. Those who have contributed are identified in the text, and their publications are cited in full in the Bibliography at the end of the book.

In Atlanta, we want to thank the various members of the Argenbright organization with whom we worked, and in particular Frank Argenbright, who brought us both to the honesty testing field. His dedication to our own research, and his support, are appreciated very much.

In Eugene, we owe a special debt to Lewis Goldberg of the University of Oregon and the Oregon Research Institute, who earlier chaired the American Psychological Association task force on honesty testing. Lew reviewed our whole manuscript in draft form and provided us with detailed comments page by page. His contribution has been enormous. We want to emphasize that the final product is ours, not his, and that he should not be held responsible for the shortcomings in that product. But we also want to acknowledge the many hours of hard work he put in, and thank him for that work.

At Quorum we have had assistance from several editors who have helped to make this book possible and to shape its final form. These are Marcy Weiner, Eric Valentine, and Lynn Taylor. We appreciate the help all have given us.

Finally, throughout the years of our work in the honesty testing field Barbara Miner has been heavily involved. She has conducted statistical analyses, edited and typed reports, put this manuscript in a form ready for publication, and helped in just about every way imaginable. In addition to ourselves, she is the only person who has contributed to this project from the very beginning. She probably knows it better than we do, and she may well have spent more time working on it. Without her efforts, *How Honesty Testing Works* would not exist.

J.B.M.
Eugene, Oregon

M.H.C.
Cropwell, Alabama

Introduction

A company that sends its personnel into the homes of clients to provide care and medical treatment had never given thought to screening for honesty. Then an employee of the company murdered a patient while in the process of stealing money and valuables from a home to which she had been sent to provide assistance. The family of the murder victim brought suit against the company for negligence. Faced with the prospect of paying sizable damages, and now aware that this type of problem could well arise again in the future, the company began to look into ways of screening prospective employees to weed out those who might prove dishonest. Inquiries at other companies indicated that polygraph testing might have been considered several years ago, but with the passage of the Polygraph Protection Act of 1988 this was no longer an alternative. Thus the company settled on honesty testing of all candidates for jobs which involved going into client homes.

WHAT IS AN HONESTY TEST?

Honesty tests are paper-and-pencil instruments (or sometimes computerized versions of such instruments) that are intended to provide an indication of how honest a person is. The terms ''honesty test'' and ''integrity test'' are often used interchangeably, although the integrity label covers a somewhat broader range of behaviors. The fact is that neither designation is entirely appropriate. To understand what is involved one has to go to the items themselves to see what factors they consider.

Study of a number of instruments yields the following list of factors:

Dishonesty and untrustworthiness
Substance abuse (both drugs and alcohol)

Deception and misrepresentation

Violent behavior and hostility

Emotional instability and maladjustment

Job instability (proclivity for rapid turnover)

Employee theft

A lack of conscientiousness in job performance

Unreliability and undependability

Inventory shrinkage

An organizational climate favoring dishonesty

Failure to accept authority and company policy

Alienated attitudes

Excessive absenteeism

Poor work ethic and values

A lack of safety consciousness

A somewhat different type of listing is provided in the *Model Guidelines for Preemployment Integrity Testing Programs*, developed by the Task Force on Integrity Testing Practices of the Association of Personnel Test Publishers:

Theft of cash, merchandise and property

Damaging merchandise to buy it on discount

Unauthorized work break extensions

"Time" theft

Repeatedly coming to work late

Coming to work with a hangover or intoxicated

Selling illicit drugs at work

Breaking rules

Damage and waste

Preventable accidents

Misuse of discount privileges

Getting paid for more hours than worked

Turnover for cause

Unauthorized use of company information

Using sick leave when not sick

On-the-job drug abuse

Intentionally doing slow or sloppy work

Gross misconduct

Vandalism

Physical assault

These are more specific behaviors, but again the range is very broad. Some tests focus on a limited set of problems, in most cases related to employee theft; some have a number of subscales dealing with different types of problems and yield subscale scores for each; some contain items dealing with a wide range of problems, but yield only a single overall score, in much the same manner as a general intelligence test does. The test on which the authors collaborated is of this latter nature. Items deal with:

Misrepresentation

Drug use on the job (and addiction)

Theft and embezzlement

Blackmail

Falsification of expenses (padding)

Excessive gambling (and addiction)

Sabotage

Time theft

Falsification of evidence

Tax fraud and cheating

Bribery

Failure to obey laws

Deliberate violations of company policy

Assault and violence

Forgery

Driving under the influence of alcohol

Lying

Sex offenses

Using alcohol on the job

Writing bad checks

It is apparent that honesty tests are much more than the label suggests. For this reason they are sometimes referred to as measures of disruptive or counterproductive behavior on the job, or of untrustworthiness. In any event we will use the term honesty test, because it appears to be the most widely used designation, but with the understanding that any or all of the factors noted in the preceding three lists may be covered under this umbrella.

TYPES OF TESTS

Honesty tests derive from two distinct origins. The earliest source was polygraph examiners who found that many of their questions did not require the presence of physiological measures and equipment to elicit confessions. The second source was psychology and the field of personality testing. In current honesty testing these streams have largely merged so that existing tests typically contain items that derive from both orientations.

In their book *Honesty and Integrity Testing: A Practical Guide* (1989), Michael O'Bannon, Linda Goldinger, and Gavin Appleby note that most test items may be classified as eliciting one of four types of responses:

Admission of illegal or disapproved activities (confessions);

Opinions toward illegal or disapproved behavior (honesty attitudes);

Descriptions of one's own personality and thought patterns (self reports); and

Reactions to hypothetical situations (scenarios). (p. 18)

Their book, although no longer up-to-date, is the most comprehensive and objective treatment of honesty testing available, and the authors' coverage of the types of items utilized appears to be adequate, even today.

Any given test may incorporate several item types. However, there do appear to be two distinct types of tests in the market, characterized, at least at the extremes, by different measurement approaches. Writing in the journal *Personnel Psychology* (1989), Paul Sackett, Laura Burris, and Christine Callahan label these as overt integrity and personality-based tests. Overt measures (also called clear-purpose) leave no question that they are aimed at finding out about dishonesty; they use items dealing with confessions and honesty attitudes.

Personality-based tests (also called personality-oriented and veiled—or disguised—purpose) use items of a kind more commonly employed in personality measurement generally. They are intended to measure personality characteristics related to honesty broadly defined, such as conscientiousness, trouble with authority, thrill seeking, nonconformity, dependability, and the like. Self-report items might include "You are more sensible than adventurous," "You work hard and steady at whatever you undertake," "You love to take chances," and "You never would talk back to a boss or a teacher." Such items do not necessarily alert the test-taker as to what is being measured.

Although at the extremes overt integrity and personality-based tests can be quite different, presumably reflecting their origins in polygraph testing and personality testing respectively, the melding of the two orientations to the field has brought with it a tendency to combine items of both types. Thus personality-based measures may contain items that are much more obvious in their intent to focus on honesty concerns as well.

HOW ARE HONESTY TESTS USED?

In the example at the beginning of the introduction, the company adopted honesty testing as a means of screening out undesirable applicants. This is by far the most common use. In some instances an honesty test is given first, and those who do not do sufficiently well on it are eliminated from further consideration. This reduces hiring costs because other selection instruments including interviews need not be introduced, but it places a heavy burden on the honesty test. Alternatively the honesty test may be used as a hurdle later in the selection process, after some applicants already have been weeded out by other procedures, or it may be included among a number of selection components that all applicants undergo.

A second use is with employees who are currently on the payroll. Honesty testing may be introduced in connection with the investigation of a crime, much as polygraph testing would be used. Absent a confession, it is unlikely that this type of testing will actually identify a thief, but it can narrow down the list of likely perpetrators, and thus make the investigation easier to conduct. There are honesty tests specifically designed for this purpose.

Another application with current employees involves consideration for promotion or transfer. If a person is a candidate for movement into a job where the opportunity for dishonest acts is greater and surveillance is more difficult, companies may introduce honesty testing prior to making these placement decisions. Here the issues are much the same as in hiring except that the people involved, being already employed, cannot as easily be sent packing if test performance is not up to par.

Finally, companies have used honesty tests in connection with comprehensive surveys of company personnel to get at the overall climate for theft, drug use, and other honesty test factors. Periodic reviews of this kind can get at changes over time, and they can help to provide solid evidence on issues that were previously only a matter of individual impression and thus the subject of considerable, fruitless debate. In this instance the actual name of the individual employee need not be known, and in fact many of these surveys are conducted anonymously.

WHAT IS THE AUDIENCE FOR HONESTY TESTING?

Although honesty testing in some form dates back at least 50 years, widespread usage is of much more recent origin. It was not until retail stores and financial institutions came to view the tests as providing protection against theft and shrinkage, which could not otherwise be controlled, that a true honesty testing industry began to develop. It remains true today that retail clerks and bank employees constitute the major audience for honesty testing. Any job where the employee has an opportunity to steal money or product because other control systems are difficult to administer effectively is a candidate for honesty testing of this kind.

This raises a question regarding supervisory and management positions. Many such positions present the same opportunity for theft, or embezzlement. At the lower levels honesty tests are widely used, but further up in the management hierarchy they are used less often. The difficulty is that companies often anticipate that the tests, especially overt integrity tests, will scare away talent that is in short supply. One solution is to focus on the more disguised personality-based instruments. Another is to embed the honesty test in a comprehensive test battery where it may appear less objectionable.

The expansion of honesty testing beyond the confines of employee theft also has affected the audience. A glance at the three lists of factors covered by the tests noted previously will indicate immediately that many of the problems relate to aspects of almost any job. The focus now is not on a few jobs in certain industries where theft is particularly likely. Instead the concern is with substance abuse, violence, job instability, excessive absenteeism, vandalism, policy violations, and the like which can emerge in any type of work. To the extent that these aspects of employee performance are incorporated in an honesty test the audience for the test expands dramatically.

Certainly the demise of polygraph testing in recent years has contributed to the expanded audience for honesty tests, but so too has the expanded range of job behaviors that these tests cover. They have simply been increasingly responsive to the demands of the marketplace.

The audience is influenced as well by the person who makes the decision to adopt honesty testing, or who exercises substantial impact on that decision. Identifying those who are part of the decision network when honesty tests are adopted is important.

Larger firms with human resource departments are more likely to employ psychologists who will champion honesty tests, and they are also more likely to have security managers who may do the same. In the one instance, the tie between honesty tests and personality testing seems to be key; in the latter, the tie with polygraph testing is more important. This split influence can produce conflict within the decision process as well, usually as to what type of test should be used. On occasion, however, psychologists may be unconvinced as to the value of honesty tests and security managers may find them unacceptable substitutes for the polygraph. There can be a lot of organizational politics involved.

Yet large firms with human resource, and perhaps separate security, departments are far from being the whole audience. As indicated in *Human Resource Management: The Strategic Perspective* by John Miner and Donald Crane (1995), power over human resource issues may reside in many places in an organization. Thus decisions regarding honesty testing may be made in the human resource or security departments, but they may be made in many other places as well.

Professional firms tend to leave control over such matters to senior professionals. This would be true in such organizations as law firms and many hospitals. Companies devoted to empowering lower level employees and introducing participative systems at lower levels may place decisions of this kind in the hands of the group. In smaller firms there often is no human resource, or security, department, and human resource decisions fall to the owner/manager or another person such as the controller. An article by Patricia Smith in *HR Magazine* (1991) documents this situation.

The point is that power over decisions regarding honesty testing may reside in many places in an organization, depending on who has that power, who wishes to exercise it, and who delegates it to whom. This situation presents a major problem for those who sell honesty tests, because it is often difficult to know what person to contact within a firm. Yet it also seems likely to contribute to a larger potential audience as well. From the company viewpoint the key consideration is that the person possess and use the most relevant knowledge, so that an effective decision is reached. Given the great variability among firms, there can be no certainty as to what person that will be.

THE PURPOSE OF THIS BOOK

The audience for this book is made up of those people who make decisions regarding honesty testing for their firms, wherever they may be located. Our perspective is not that of governmental regulating bodies or professional associations, or test publishers, or labor unions, or citizen action groups (such as the American Civil Liberties Union), but only of those companies that might reasonably utilize honesty tests for economic purposes such as increased productivity, growth, expanded sales, and greater profits. We recognize the concerns and expectations of individual employees and potential employees, and we will give expression to these considerations at various points. Nevertheless, our overall focus is more global, at the company level. That is the level that we feel needs the greatest attention at the present time, and it is the level at which we are most qualified to offer guidance.

In *The Fractured Marketplace for Standardized Testing* (1993), authors Walter Haney, George Madaus, and Robert Lyons set forth a number of strategies for improving testing practices. They note such approaches as greater reliance on the market, professional standards and peer review, litigation, government regulation, an independent auditing agency, and the development of new kinds of tests and assessment strategies. However, the approach with the most relevance for this book is greater education of test users. Haney, Madaus, and Lyons are not particularly optimistic regarding the value of this strategy, in part because so many people use different types of tests for different purposes. Yet, if the audience is limited to employers and their representatives using tests for purposes of hiring employees and operating an organization, as it can be in the case of honesty tests, there seems to be greater reason for optimism. Thus the purpose of this book is to assist in the education of honesty test users so that they can make informed decisions.

In undertaking this objective, we have decided not to deal with specific tests by name; our approach is essentially generic. The reason is that new instruments arrive in the marketplace regularly, and some disappear as well. It is impossible to be completely up-to-date, and in any event we do not have the detailed information on all tests currently in the market that would permit us to make relative value judgments. Thus our aim is to arm our readers with sufficient information and knowledge to make these value judgments for themselves.

THE MATTER OF OBJECTIVITY

Honesty testing is a business—a very competitive business with many players involved. Much of the research and writing in the field stems from those who market tests. Consequently, questions have arisen regarding the fuzzy borderline between scientific research and aggressive selling. How independent and objective is a given study or publication? This is not an issue unique to honesty testing. It is inherent in much industrial research and development (R&D) as well. Nevertheless, it is a problem that needs to be addressed.

Increasingly, those writing on the subject of honesty testing have adopted a policy of revealing their past and present associations within the industry, or the lack thereof, so that readers can take this information into account. Examples are the disclosure statements contained in O'Bannon, Goldinger, and Appleby (1989) and Sackett, Burris, and Callahan (1989). In addition, this issue is given attention in a paper by Dan Dalton, Michael Metzger, and James Wimbush entitled "Integrity Testing for Personnel Selection: A Review and Research Agenda" which appeared in *Research in Personnel and Human Resources Management* (1994). Ira Morrow (1992) raises similar concerns in his *Personnel Psychology* book review of John Jones' *Preemployment Honesty Testing: Current Research and Future Directions* (1991).

It has become quite apparent that those writing in the honesty testing field need to provide information on their association with the industry, especially if they are doing some type of review or survey that presupposes an objective approach and balanced coverage. Since this is in many respects such a survey of the honesty testing literature, and an analysis of its implications for users, we feel it is incumbent on us to provide some type of disclosure statement.

Both of the authors worked together for over five years developing, conducting research and development studies on, and marketing an honesty test of the overt or clear-purpose type. The parent company involved had as its core business the provision of security and the detection of crime, including the conduct of polygraph examinations. As it became evident that some type of restrictive federal polygraph legislation might pass, the owner of the company decided to hedge his investments by diversifying into honesty testing. His reasoning was that if other polygraph firms could bridge the gap into psychological testing successfully, and several had, he could as well. Miner was hired in the early period as an outside consultant to assist in developing such a test. Capps served initially as president of the polygraph subsidiary, and after the honesty test was published became the president of the subsidiary established to market the test.

The honesty test was sold to users over a five-year period. Although initially quite successful, the test never actually fulfilled its owner's expectations. There were a series of crises. It was difficult to develop new markets in a business climate where customers were concerned that honesty testing would be restricted in the same manner as polygraph testing had been. They waited first for the report entitled *The Use of Integrity Tests for Pre-employment Screening* prepared by the Office of Technology Assessment of the U.S. Congress, which finally appeared in September 1990; then they waited until February 1991 for the task force report from the American Psychological Association (Goldberg et al.) entitled *Questionnaires Used in the Prediction of Trustworthiness in Pre-employment Selection Decisions*. Negative reports from these two sources had combined to have a major impact on the passage of the Polygraph Protection Act of 1988. Would they do the same again in the case of honesty tests?

Subsequent crises producing the need for major revisions in the test came with the passage of the Civil Rights Act of 1991, and then later as the Americans with Disabilities Act went into effect. Ultimately the owner decided that further investment in the test was not warranted, and it was removed from the market.

As of this writing, the authors have had no financial involvement with the honesty testing industry for over two-and-a-half years. We learned a great deal from our previous experiences in the business and we conducted a number of studies that will be used throughout this book to illustrate points that need to be made. However, the test is no longer being marketed, and we have no ties to that or any other honesty testing business. Thus we are free to make an objective presentation on the subject. Clearly our previous experiences have influenced us, but there are no current monetary influences; we are not selling anything (except this book).

1

Why Honesty Tests Have Become So Popular

We do not know how many employers use honesty tests of some type, or how many tests are administered in any given year. Estimates in the literature would suggest some 5,000 to 6,000 firms use the tests and the number tested is in the 2.5 to 5 million range. However, these figures are all outdated, some by as much as 10 years or more. In the period since the figures were generated the Polygraph Protection Act has taken hold, various controversies that had a damping effect on the market at least for the moment have been resolved, and the psychological community has come to have a more favorable perception of the tests. As Walter Haney, George Madaus, and Robert Lyons (1993) note, ''The one realm in which employment testing clearly seems to have increased sharply in recent years is with respect to pencil and paper honesty testing'' (p. 89). Although this growth is spread across employment sectors, it appears most pronounced in wholesale and retail trade.

At any given time there would seem to be something like 50 tests on the market, often with several different versions available. There are almost as many honesty test publishers. These publishers have been rather secretive in the past, although many are now becoming more open, and sales figures are impossible to obtain in most cases. In spite of the large number of tests available, however, it appears that the three larger publishers have at least 50 percent of the market, and by some estimates as much as 70 percent; thus there is a substantial degree of concentration in the industry. The Michael O'Bannon, Linda Goldinger, and Gavin Appleby (1989) volume contains a good discussion of the extent and nature of the honesty testing industry up through the 1980s.

Although this brief review is far from definitive regarding just *how* popular the procedure is, there is no question that honesty testing does possess considerable popularity, especially in certain business sectors. Furthermore, the forecast for the future looks strong; continued growth appears likely. We need, then, to develop an understanding of why this popularity has occurred. What problems are honesty tests thought to solve?

THE THEFT PROBLEM

Historically, honesty tests were first developed to deal with theft problems, and that appears to remain their primary use today. To the extent that theft by employees, especially the more severe forms of theft, is widespread in organizations, the size of the problem is more extensive, and thus the greater the need for methods of dealing with it.

The definition of severe theft is a matter of judgment. A study conducted by Michael Boye and Karen Slora reported in the *Journal of Business and Psychology* (1993) considers this matter, based on the opinions of a group of security experts. In order of severity, the following types of behaviors were emphasized:

1. Took money from employer without permission.
2. Took merchandise or equipment from employer without permission.
3. Changed company records to get paid for work not actually done.
4. Issued or received refunds for things not actually purchased.
5. Took personal property from co-workers.
6. Actively helped another person take company property and/or merchandise.
7. Faked injury to receive worker's compensation.
8. Falsified a company document for personal gain.
9. Overcharged or shortchanged customers on purpose.
10. Sold merchandise to friends at reduced prices.
11. Did not report a theft of company cash or merchandise by another employee.

This listing of severe theft-related behaviors was developed for the supermarket industry. In other industries the specific behaviors might rank somewhat differently and take different forms. However, these are certainly among the behaviors likely to be considered when serious employee theft is discussed.

Because this supermarket industry study focused on lower-level employees, it appears not to have given sufficient weight to certain forms of white collar theft. An article by Laurel Touby appearing in the *Journal of Business Strategy* (1994) redresses this imbalance. Over a 10-year period, arrests for fraud have gone up 25 percent and for embezzlement 56 percent. According to a recent Peat, Marwick study, 76 percent of the companies surveyed had experienced fraud within the past year, with the median cost to each firm being $200,000. Most often small amounts of money are taken over a period of time. In a two-year period, for example, an employee of the Federal Deposit Insurance Corporation (FDIC) took $45,000 by forging receipts and signatures on petty cash vouchers. The most he could have taken at any one time was $100.

Valid figures on the overall loss to companies from some type of theft and the proportion of employees involved are not easily obtained. In his book *Honesty in the Workplace* (1993), Kevin Murphy reports annual dollar values ranging from 4 billion to 200 billion. These figures reflect varying definitions of theft, varying degrees of guesswork in the estimates, and the influence of inflation (more recent figures are higher). At present it probably would not be grossly incorrect to use a value of $100 billion, although the potential for error in that figure remains high. Smaller businesses are particularly vulnerable; as much as 30 percent of business failures among small firms appears to be occasioned at least in part by internal theft.

While estimates of the dollar amounts involved vary widely, estimates of the proportion of employees involved exhibit more consistency. The best data appear to come from studies utilizing reports from employees themselves obtained via anonymous surveys. An extensive study of this kind described in *Theft by Employees* by Richard Hollinger and John Clark (1983) indicated that from 28 to 35 percent of employees, depending on the industry, participated in significant theft in a given year. A similar study by Karen Slora in the *Journal of Business and Psychology* (1989) produced a figure of 43 percent (35 percent severe) in a group of retail supermarkets, but among employees in the fast-food industry a value of over 60 percent was obtained.

Clearly there are substantial variations in theft across jobs and industries, depending in large part on the opportunities available. In retail sales, where employees handle money, theft is more prevalent—in part because the temptation exists, but also because the existence of opportunity attracts those who wish to steal.

Another factor contributing to variations in the figures is the dishonesty climate perceived by the employees of an organization. Some companies are perceived by their employees as particularly permissive or lenient when it comes to theft, while others are perceived as more strict. This factor makes a substantial difference in terms of the amount of theft occurring, as John Kamp and Paul Brooks, writing in the *Journal of Business and Psychology* (1991), have shown. A company, through the way it acts and presents itself, can appear to be inviting theft. This would seem to be particularly likely when those in top-level positions are engaged in some type of white collar crime.

Theft rates are also affected by the extent to which employees feel management has treated them unfairly. This is nicely demonstrated in a study by Jerald Greenberg published in the *Journal of Applied Psychology* (1990), which compared three plants in the same company with regard to inventory shrinkage during a period when lost contracts necessitated a 15 percent temporary pay cut in two of the plants. In the plant where the pay cut was simply announced with little justification and no apology, the theft index rose sharply. In the plant where top management spent considerable time both explaining and apologizing, theft increased, but to a level less than half of that found in the first plant. In the third plant, production was unaffected by the lost contracts and accordingly no pay reduction occurred; here theft levels remained low and unchanged. Subsequent research conducted by Greenberg and presented in *Organizational Behavior and Human Decision Processes* (1993) makes it clear that providing a valid explanation and responding with understanding and sensitivity can indeed reduce theft, but still does not eliminate it. In situations where employees believe that an employer has defaulted on its obligations and broken its promises, theft apparently becomes a means of making up the difference, thus compensating for the inequity.

For all of these reasons, a given employer may experience theft rates that deviate considerably from the national average. Accordingly, honesty testing to reduce theft would seem to have much more justification in certain contexts than in others.

DRUG AND ALCOHOL PROBLEMS

Former U.S. Secretary of Labor Lynn Martin, writing in *HR Focus* (1992) notes that substance abuse in the workplace contributes to much greater use of medical benefits, substantially increased absenteeism, and a doubling of workers' compensation claims. This is in addition to the decrease in on-the-job productivity. Alcohol consumption is a major source of accidents, and consequently injuries and death. Studies by Siegfried Streufert and his colleagues published in the *Journal of Applied Psychology* (1992) show that error rates increase dramatically with alcohol consumption and the capacity to deal with crises is greatly diminished. Michael McDaniel in *Personnel Psychology* (1988) reports on a variety of job-related effects of drug use, all of them negative.

Comprehensive reviews of the literature on substance abuse as it relates to the work environment are contained in an article by Michael Harris and Laura Heft in the *Journal of Management* (1992) and in an article by Russell Cropanzano and Mary Konovsky in *Research in Personnel and Human Resources Management* (1993). Again, anonymous self-report studies appear to yield the most satisfactory conclusions. Although test-positive rates for drug testing of current employees have consistently remained under 5 percent, this percentage represents a substantial underestimate of the problem; companies that test tend to drive out drug users. On-the-job drug use among younger workers appears to run closer to 10 percent, and in specific situations rates as high as 30 percent have been reported. Alcohol use at work appears to represent a problem of at least the same magnitude, and may well be even more frequent. The best available cost estimates for substance abuse indicate a figure that now exceeds $100 billion including lost productivity. These are, however, only estimates.

According to data reported by Philip Gleason and his colleagues in the *Monthly Labor Review* (1991) both drug and alcohol problems are the most acute in the construction industry, and in entertainment and recreation. Rates in wholesale and retail trade are not as severely elevated. Yet it remains true that many employees who create the substance abuse problem steal from their employers as well, often to obtain drugs and alcohol. In many instances the two types of problems go hand in hand, partly because the two tend to exist in the same people, and partly because company permissiveness is extended to cover both types of behavior.

PRODUCTION DEVIANCE AND SABOTAGE

In their book *Theft by Employees* (1983), Hollinger and Clark define production deviance to include taking a long lunch or break without approval, coming to work late or leaving early, using sick leave when one is not sick, and doing slow or sloppy work intentionally. Such behaviors are often labeled ''time theft,'' although they may well extend beyond that. They are frequent in that from 60 to 80 percent of employees in different work settings report them. Yet they are not typically viewed as severe as long as they do not occur often. Nevertheless, the overall loss to employers can be considerable, simply because so many employees are involved. If something can be done to screen out those with the greatest likelihood of engaging in production deviance, companies can benefit in many ways. At the same time it needs to be recognized that much of this behavior occurs because the firm is lax in enforcing its policies and procedures. Permissiveness can contribute as much as the type of person. There is a relation between production deviance and theft, however. Employees who are heavily involved in one may be more likely to be involved in the other as well.

Sabotage is closely related to production deviance, but it is more deliberate. Michael Crino and Terry Leap, writing in *Personnel* (1989), describe it as deliberate behavior intended to damage company property, tarnish the company reputation, or subvert company operations. It is normally premeditated. Increasingly, it has involved computer operations. Thus it includes destruction of machinery or goods, but it can also include stopping and slowing down production. In a study of unionized workers conducted by Robert Giacalone and Paul Rosenfeld published in the *Journal of Business and Psychology* (1987), the reasons for sabotage noted in decreasing order of frequency were (1) to protect one's job, (2) self-defense, (3) to protect friends and family from a boss or the company, (4) to similarly protect oneself, and (5) ''an eye for an eye.'' Clearly retribution is a major consideration. The forms of action reported, in order of the extent to which they were considered most justified, were calling upon the union to intervene, carrying out management directives to the letter, doing personal work on company time with company tools and supplies, punching someone else's time card (or the reverse), creating work slow downs, creating down time, going to the clinic to get away from work, and at the least justified end slowing down work output to get a supervisor in trouble or fired. The more extreme versions such as damaging machinery and bomb threats were not generally considered to be justified, but it is evident that they sometimes do occur.

Sabotage seems most frequent in the face of layoffs, downsizing, mergers and acquisitions, and union campaigns—when some justification can be established. Yet it is very difficult to say how frequent this type of sabotage is. What is known may very well be "the tip of the iceberg."

It is also evident that computer installations create a special opportunity for sabotage. A recently fired employee who worked in a large mainframe computer site got revenge on her former employer by returning to the computer center to "clean out her desk." She carried a large briefcase and made sure to stop in the tape library, by the disk storage units, and by the tape drives. Unfortunately for the company, she had a large iron bar wrapped in wire and connected to several dry-cell batteries in the briefcase. The large electromagnet radiated a magnetic field large enough to scramble tapes and jumble disk drive units. In another organization, a staff member changed large amounts of data in the system and altered the formulas used to compute paychecks.

WORKPLACE VIOLENCE

The following news release appeared in December 1994 in the *Buffalo News*:

A disgruntled auto worker, fearing he was about to be fired, shot and killed his supervisor at a Chrysler Corp. factory Friday and seriously wounded another worker, police said.

According to police and witnesses at the plant in the Detroit suburb of Sterling Heights, Clarence Woods, 48, got into an argument with another worker, pulled a .38-caliber gun and shot the supervisor when he tried to intervene.

He then reloaded his weapon and continued firing until he was out of ammunition.

When he was done, witnesses said he kicked the supervisor several times, sat down and waited for police to arrive.

Willie Ruffin, 54, of Detroit died in the attack and employee Ed Williams, 65, was injured, said John Danski, president of Local 1264.

Sterling Heights Police Chief Thomas Derocha said the gunman had been involved in an assault in 1993.

Woods' co-workers said he was on probation and afraid of losing his job.

An unidentified eyewitness told WJBK-TV the gunman had a history of mood swings.

Some of the people who worked with Woods felt these moods were the major cause of the shooting. Others implicated the stress of heavy overtime work, and the fact that there was a history of conflict within the group. This was the second shooting in a Detroit auto plant over the last three months. In Dearborn, at Ford's Rouge plant, an official of the United Auto Workers killed two fellow committeemen and wounded two more during an argument over union policies. Oliver French, an electrician at the Rouge plant for 28 years, has been charged with the shootings.

Murder on the job is not a common event, although there is reason to believe it is becoming more frequent. However, violence of some kind is much more widespread, and it can carry with it substantial costs. The following quote from an article by Robert Elliott and Deborah Jarrett in *Public Personnel Management* (1994) describes some of these:

There are the immediate costs of human pain, suffering, and possible loss of life. There is the cost of traumatized employees, families of employees, and co-workers that can never be properly put into financial terms. Beyond these human losses, there are the more concrete costs to the organization brought about by legal liabilities for death, injuries, and traumatic stress. These losses will involve repayment to employees through worker's compensation benefits, counseling, or medical care. Legal fees to defer the costs of litigation resulting from homicide type events can be sources of enormous costs. Beyond this, there may be jury awards to employees, families, and victims. Loss of productivity from employees is another cost component that must be considered. Revenue losses from lowered levels of productivity, the inability to retain good employees, and future problems in the area of recruitment may also be costs related to such a violent event in the workplace. (p. 288)

Workplace violence taken to the extreme means murder, but it includes a number of behaviors that to varying degrees fall short of the extreme, including threats of violence. Among these are attacks, assaults, and fights involving customers, other employees, and supervisors; anger-related accidents; rapes and certain types of sexual harassment; unauthorized use of any kind of weapon; and arson. According to figures provided by Dawn Anfuso in a recent *Personnel Journal* article (1994), in a one-year period 2.2 million workers are physically attacked on the job and 6.3 million are threatened with violence. Incidents of this type are said to cost employers $4 billion annually in lost work and legal expenses alone. Again we need to emphasize the potential for error in these figures.

Clearly workplace violence can occur in any type of position. Homicides tend to be particularly concentrated in taxicab establishments, liquor stores, gas stations, detective or protection agencies, justice and public order establishments, grocery stores, jewelry stores, hotels and motels, and eating and drinking establishments. As with theft, retail trade positions experience more than their share. For some reason certain organizations seem to attract violence more than others. Since 1986, as of this writing, 38 people have been killed and 20 wounded in 12 U.S. Post Office shootings; most of this violence was at the hands of co-workers or former co-workers.

One key to understanding this kind of attraction for violence derives from a report in the *Journal of Occupational and Organizational Psychology* on research conducted by Peter Chen and Paul Spector (1992). They found that various sources of stress in the workplace were related to the potential for violence among employees. Where stress was high, violence was more likely. Others have attributed the rise in workplace violence to the stress created by downsizing and mergers. These types of explanations seem to argue that pre-hiring selection would be unlikely to solve the problem. However, some people are known to be much more responsive to the kinds of stresses that occur at work than others. If honesty tests given prior to hiring can identify such people and either preclude them from employment or signal a need for placement in low-stress types of jobs, part of the workplace violence problem might be reduced.

Two recent articles in *Business Horizons*, one by Romuald Stone (1995) and the other by Michael Harvey and Richard Cosier (1995), provide a good overview of steps companies may take to deal with workplace violence.

LEGAL LIABILITIES INVOLVING NEGLIGENCE

Theft, drug and alcohol problems, production deviance, sabotage, and violence all can create major difficulties for companies in their workplaces, escalating costs and decreasing profits, sometimes to a point where the company is put out of business entirely. These considerations contribute substantially to the popularity of honesty tests. However, an additional factor is the legal liability that honesty testing may serve to reduce. Companies may introduce honesty testing to minimize liability both by preventing behavior that provokes litigation and by demonstrating a good-faith effort to deal with problems that might create legal liabilities. Workplace violence is most likely to be involved in such cases, but widespread drug and alcohol abuse can serve to produce threats to safety sufficient to introduce legal concerns as well. Edward Miller in *HR Magazine* (1991) describes how Tri Valley Growers in California became concerned about safety in the face of extensive drug abuse at work, and took steps to deal with the problem. Even theft may constitute a basis for legal action.

Yet violence is the prime concern. A state court in Colorado ordered McDonald's to pay damages after a developmentally disabled worker sexually assaulted a three-year-old boy at a restaurant. The employee had a history of sexually assaulting children, but McDonald's was unaware of the conviction history. The court found that the state agency that placed the worker and McDonald's shared liability for the negligent hire.

A case in Florida involved a woman whose husband was killed by a fellow bank guard. The killer had previously given numerous indications of mental illness, but the bank continued to employee him as a security guard. The widow sued the bank for negligent hiring and won a substantial judgment.

In Minnesota an apartment manager with a passkey entered a woman's apartment and raped her. The manager had a history of violent crime convictions. The court found that the investment company that owned the apartments had a duty to exercise reasonable care in hiring individuals who, because of their employment, may pose a threat of injury to the public. The company was ordered to pay a sizable settlement to the woman because of its negligence in this regard.

The legal reasoning in cases of these kinds is set forth in an article by James Quirk in *HR Magazine* (1993), and in greater detail by Ann Ryan and Marja Lasek in the journal *Personnel Psychology* (1991):

1. An injury must be shown to be caused by an employee acting within the *employment relationship.*

2. The employee must be shown to be *unfit or incompetent* in some manner.

3. The employer must be shown to have prior knowledge of this unfitness or it must be proven that the employer *should have known* about the problem.

4. The injury must be shown to have been caused by the *employee's act or omission.*

5. The employer's *negligence* in hiring or retaining the employee must be shown to be the *most likely cause* of the injuries.

A sufficient number of cases have been brought, and won, on these grounds that employers need to be, and typically are, concerned. Judgments can be in the millions of dollars. Honesty testing may be judged to be a means of establishing certain types of unfitness, and thus of preventing negligent hiring.

THE EROSION OF "EMPLOYMENT-AT-WILL"

For a number of reasons it seems best for an employer to discover an honesty problem via testing prior to employment, rather than facing the need for discharge later on. Discharge is becoming more difficult, and more costly as well. Under an employment-at-will doctrine an employer can discharge an employee for a good cause, a bad cause, or no cause at all unless an existing employment contract limits this right. For many years this was the law of the land. However, more and more of this land is being eroded.

Union contracts have increasingly contained provisions that terminations can occur only for "just cause," and many non-union companies now have come to accept this terminology as well. This means that an employer must prove a reason for discharge. The difficulty of accomplishing this is reflected in the fact that some 75 percent of cases involving theft that go to arbitration are overturned by the arbitrator, with reinstatement being the usual remedy.

Second, civil rights and labor laws have made it much easier to claim that a discharge is unwarranted because it was based on sex, race, color, religion, national origin, age, union activity, handicap, or in some cases sexual orientation. The result has been a substantial bite out of employment-at-will.

Third, courts have increasingly recognized a concept of wrongful discharge. This concept involves three exceptions to employment-at-will which are set forth in a *Journal of Small Business Management* article by Glenn Gomes and James Morgan (1992). One is a public policy exception, when a termination undermines some important societal interest (refusing to commit an unlawful act, performing a public obligation such as jury duty, or exercising a basic right such as voting). A second exception involves a much expanded view of what constitutes an implied employment contract; job security may be implied simply by long duration of employment. Finally, a termination may be judged to violate good faith and fair dealing, as when an employee is separated to avoid paying pension benefits; this last exception can be interpreted very broadly.

Various states apply these exceptions differently, but there can be no doubt that employment-at-will is under attack and on the defensive. There are several ways of dealing with this dilemma, none of which is universally effective, but screening out employees who may have to be separated later is an attractive option. At the least, this approach saves a company from needing to prove in a court of law that a separation was justified (although there is always the possibility that under certain circumstances the refusal to hire may need to be justified). Honesty testing thus can be attractive as a protection against downside litigation related to erosion of employment-at-will, as well as against negligent hiring liabilty.

CONCLUSIONS

How large are the problems considered in this chapter? Probably the best way of stating the matter is in terms of the numbers of employees involved. Yet it is not appropriate to simply add up the number heavily involved in theft, in drug and alcohol abuse, in production deviance and sabotage, and in violence. As we have seen there are correlations among these factors, often substantial correlations, so that the same person who contributes to one type of problem may well contribute to several others also.

One approach is to consider the results obtained from pre-employment polygraph screening before the Polygraph Protection Act became law. We will take up the polygraph in greater detail in the next chapter, but it is sufficient to note that it is intended to identify the full range of problems under consideration. In our experience roughly 35 percent of those tested exhibit no problems of any kind on the polygraph, and another 15 percent exhibit problems that are not of sufficient magnitude and/or recency to be considered severe. Another 10 percent give evidence of a serious problem, but that problem is restricted to one specific type such as theft or drug use. Finally, a full 40 percent appear to be involved in severe and pervasive problem behaviors.

These figures come from business settings where the problems are particularly frequent, and the consequences serious; that is why the firms involved, many of them in retail trade, paid to have polygraph investigations. Nevertheless, the polygraph data fit well with the figures reported elsewhere in this chapter. A large number of firms do face serious problems. This is no straw man (or woman). For those who may have remaining doubts regarding the extent of the problem, we suggest reading *Cheats at Work: An Anthropology of Workplace Crime* by Gerald Mars (1994). This book contains the results of extensive first-hand observations showing how, and how widely, workplace crime operates.

Furthermore, the legal climate has evolved in a direction that argues strongly for the need to protect oneself against claims of negligence and unfair discharge. In later chapters of this book, we will take up a number of legal considerations that have created difficulties for honesty testing. However, it is apparent that the law can cut both ways. Certain laws, and the way they have been interpreted by the courts, do seem to argue for the use of something like honesty testing.

Honesty testing has become popular in large part as a result of the problems treated in this chapter. But a number of other approaches to these problems have become popular too, or at least appear to have the potential to help solve them. What are the relative merits of these alternatives? Are there not other ways than honesty testing to achieve the same results? These are the issues to be considered in the next chapter.

2

What Are the Alternatives to Honesty Testing?

Different professionals come to the problems associated with employee honesty with different approaches and skills. Accountants tend to emphasize financial control systems including audits. Internal security personnel are likely to stress surveillance and investigation. Organizational behavior specialists may well attempt to improve job satisfaction and foster a climate or culture that promotes honesty.

Honesty testing can be used, as we have noted, in conjunction with these approaches to aid investigations and to measure honesty climate or culture. However, its major purpose is not to cope with problems created by those already hired, but rather to screen out those who are likely to create these problems, so that they never are employed in the first place. It is the alternatives available for this purpose that are considered in this chapter. In addition to polygraph testing these include reference checks, background investigations dealing with such factors as criminal records and credit ratings, drug testing of a physiological nature, application blanks and biodata focused on honesty, integrity interviewing, and personality assessment generally.

The Model Guidelines for Preemployment Integrity Testing (Association of Personnel Test Publishers, 1991) reviews a number of these alternatives and concludes that "professionally developed integrity tests are the most valid screening method for predicting theft criteria." We propose here to take a deeper look at issues of this kind, in an attempt to achieve a balanced judgment.

POLYGRAPH TESTING

For many years the preferred approach in a large number of organizations to identifying problems of theft, alcohol and drug use, sabotage, and violence in the work setting has been the polygraph, or lie detector. It has been very widely used where these problems are widespread and their impact on the firm likely to be severe.

The polygraph instrument simultaneously measures blood pressure and pulse, sweat gland activity, and respiratory patterns. A review of existing research carried out by Michael Capps and reported in *Polygraph* (1991) indicates that all three types of measures make important contributions to the results obtained. There do appear, however, to be other physiological measures that could be incorporated in the examination, although to date they typically have not been. For instance, Theodore Bashore and Paul Rapp, writing in *Psychological Bulletin* (1993), present encouraging evidence for the use of event-related brain potentials, which reflect the electrical activity of the brain. Yet, like almost everything said about the polygraph, this issue, too, has raised controversy, as reflected in a follow-on article by J. P. Rosenfeld writing in the same journal (1995). Nevertheless, it seems entirely possible that the polygraph of the future may not be identical to the polygraph of today.

As Michael Capps and his colleagues point out in a 1995 *Polygraph* article, even though the current polygraph is standardized as to the physiological measures obtained, the actual examination process can vary tremendously, depending on who conducts the investigation. The questions asked, the physiological responses to which are recorded, can vary widely, and so too can the methods by which various sources of data are combined to reach the final conclusion. The result is that polygraph testing is as much a consequence of the skill and experience of the examiner as it is of the instrument itself. Some authors, such as Leonard Saxe writing in *Current Directions in Psychological Science* (1994), argue that to the extent the test works at all, it is because the examiner is adept at fostering a belief that the apparatus can, in fact, detect deception.

In the hiring context, it is true that a sizable proportion of rejections occasioned by polygraph results occur because the applicant confesses at some point during the examination to some type of past problem behavior. These confessions presumably are fostered in part by a belief that the imposing apparatus is all-knowing. But they also are fostered by the skill that the examiner possesses in eliciting confessions; some are better than others. As Michael Capps and Norman Ansley, again in *Polygraph* (1992), have shown, there is no reason to believe that the physiological recordings of people known to be deceptive differ, depending on whether a confession is or is not obtained. The confession appears to be primarily a function of the skills of the examiner, not the type of person.

This matter of confession rates is particularly important in pre-employment polygraph testing. Much of the controversy over the effectiveness of polygraph investigations centers on whether the physiological measures actually do reflect deceptions. However, to the extent confessions are involved, for practical purposes an employer will have less concern over the ongoing debate. The key is to utilize examiners who can elicit confessions from those who have something to confess. In some contexts, as many as 95 percent of those who fail the polygraph are reported to have admitted to some type of wrong-doing. Our experience with day-to-day preemployment polygraph screening would indicate this figure to be too high, but not by a great deal.

A final point relates to whether the polygraph can be beaten. It has been claimed that the instrument will not work with hard-core psychopathic criminals who are accustomed to lying without blinking an eye. However, Christopher Patrick and William Iacono present evidence in the *Journal of Applied Psychology* (1989) that this is not the case; psychopathic criminals exhibit no special skills in beating the polygraph.

On the other hand there are countermeasures that with training can be used effectively to defeat the polygraph and prevent the detection of guilt. When used correctly, these countermeasures are very difficult for an examiner to detect. An article by Charles Honts, David Raskin, and John Kircher in the *Journal of Applied Psychology* (1994) provides details on what is involved. In the job selection context, very few applicants would be expected to have had the necessary training, and thus the countermeasure problem is unlikely to be of great importance. It does become important when dealing with national security clearances and intelligence agents who may have received the necessary training from the governments of other countries.

While polygraph testing is by far the best known mechanical method used in lie detection, other electronic-based methods have appeared. Among these, voice stress analysis, which relies on the assumption that the stress inherent in lying reduces involuntary frequency modulations in the human voice, requires some discussion. Robert Waln and Ronald Downey in the *Journal of Business and Psychology* (1987) review the evidence on this technique, including their own studies. They conclude that voice stress analysis does not achieve the level of effectiveness that can be attained through polygraph testing. Accordingly, the approach does not appear to be a viable alternative to honesty testing at this time.

THE IMPACT OF POLYGRAPH LEGISLATION

It appears that polygraph testing done well so as to elicit confessions, and presumably also when relying on instrument data alone under conditions where the examiner is very experienced, can be a viable alternative to honesty testing. This does not mean that there are no errors, only that like any test the probabilities favor correct prediction. In the interest of fostering a belief in the infallibility of the polygraph, some examiners have argued that they are rarely if ever wrong. That clearly is not the case. Any test that we know of is wrong sometimes, and polygraph testing is no exception. But from an employer viewpoint administering polygraphs, and using all of the information from them, can reduce the flow of problem employees into an organization.

Yet as of December 27, 1988, many employers found this alternative no longer available; the Polygraph Protection Act became law. Like much social legislation of the twentieth century, bans of various kinds on polygraph testing first occurred at the state level and then as more and more states enacted legislation this ban spread to federal law. Federal social legislation is often introduced to equalize the impact on interstate commerce across states.

The first state law restricting polygraph testing was passed by Massachusetts in 1959, and by the time the federal law was enacted roughly half of the states had some type of limitation in place. Lois Wise and Steven Charvat in *Public Personnel Management* (1990) present evidence that among states having an above average rate of labor force unionization, 19 had limits of some kind and 6 did not; among the less unionized states only 4 had such laws and 21 did not. The union movement has been a major factor in the passage of restrictive polygraph legislation at all levels of government.

Michael Capps writing in *Security Management* (1989), summarizes certain provisions of the law:

The law contains several limited exemptions that authorize private sector polygraph tests under certain conditions, including the following: 1) the testing of employees who are reasonably suspected of involvement in a workplace incident that results in economic loss or injury to the employer's business, 2) the testing of some prospective employees of private armored car, security alarm, and security guard firms, 3) the testing of some current and prospective employees in firms authorized to manufacture, distribute, or dispense controlled substances. (p. 128)

Public sector employees at the federal, state, and local levels are not covered by the act. As Capps notes, ''the government has almost completely taken away private sector use of the polygraph, while the government itself still actively uses polygraphs almost without restriction'' (p. 128). One has to wonder why, if the polygraph is so good that government cannot do without it, private sector employees must be protected from it. Or, vice versa, if the polygraph is so bad that private sector employees must be protected, why does government continue to need such a device? There is an inconsistency in the act that suggests politics rather than the public good may be behind it.

In any event, polygraph testing, as well as other mechanical or electrical approaches such as voice stress analysis, is no longer available for most pre-employment screening purposes, and the number of such tests administered has declined dramatically. It is possible that, like prohibition, the restrictive federal legislation will be lifted in time; some states might then change their laws as well. But for the present, honesty tests are an alternative to the polygraph, not the other way around.

REFERENCE CHECKING AND BACKGROUND INVESTIGATIONS

Three primary questions arise with regard to references and background investigations: (1) How good is the information obtained? (2) Do companies actually use these procedures? (3) Will people provide this type of information? With the answers to these questions, one is in a better position to judge the value of these approaches as alternatives to honesty tests.

References may be provided via letter or over the telephone. Usually the candidates provide the names, the individuals are contacted by the employer, and the information provided deals with prior employment or in some cases education. Under these circumstances most references are quite positive, with the result that there is very little differentiation among candidates, and minimal information related to honesty is unearthed. References generally have not been found to be very useful. However, regarding references provided by school principals on their students, Alan Jones and Elizabeth Harrison, writing in the *Journal of Occupational Psychology* (1982), indicate that because the principals recommended students year after year to the same sources, they came to feel considerable personal accountability for the accuracy of their reports and the results were more valid. If references can be obtained from people who consider their reputation to be on the line, this can be a useful source of information.

Background investigations go beyond references in that a number of sources are contacted, most of which are not provided by the candidate. Furthermore, as Michael McDaniel emphasized in his *Journal of Applied Psychology* (1989) article on the subject, these investigations tend to focus on the same problems as do honesty tests. An organization may utilize its own staff for this purpose, or credit investigation and detective agencies may be hired. Typically application blank data are checked out. Educational organizations are contacted, criminal records obtained if possible, credit and bankruptcy records consulted, driving histories investigated, places of residence confirmed, and friends and neighbors interviewed. To provide legal protection, a signed release needs to be obtained from the person investigated, including a waiver of liability for those providing information. If done well, these investigations can prove useful. However, *well* means comprehensive, and that tends to introduce a substantial cost.

Do companies actually use these procedures? With regard to references, the answer is clearly affirmative. Jerry Kinard and Stanley Renas, reporting in *Public Personnel Management* (1991), found average use rates across jobs for written and telephone interviews in the 75 to 80 percent range. Furthermore, a study by Sampo Paunonen, Douglas Jackson, and Steven Oberman published in *Organizational Behavior and Human Decision Processes* (1987) determined that there is a pronounced tendency to impute validity to letters of reference—people tend to believe what these letters say.

On the other hand, checks on criminal records, if they are accessible, tend to occur less than 20 percent of the time, and diplomas or licenses are evaluated with frequency only among professionals and managers. Overall, it appears that background investigations and their components are not utilized to nearly the extent that references are. In part this is due to cost, but many sources of information can be tapped directly by employers through telephone calls to appropriate agencies and organizations. The cost is minimal in these cases. Yet relatively few employers utilize these sources.

Will previous employers actually provide the needed information? Probably not. A survey conducted by Charles Langdon and William Galle, whose results are reported in *Personnel Administrator* (1989), found that on average 80 percent of the firms contacted were reluctant to provide a bad reference when an ex-employee clearly deserved one, and almost 50 percent would not supply information on documented criminal activity.

The culprit here is a charge of defamation. Any written (libelous) or oral (slanderous) communication about a former employee that harms the person in some way, where the truth of the statement cannot be documented, constitutes defamation. Statements made in references or background investigations can be of this type. The harm is that a candidate is barred from subsequent employment. Damages can be sizable. Even if the statement can be documented, legal costs may be substantial before a company clears itself.

As cases involving defamation have become more frequent and more widely publicized, companies have become less and less talkative. In certain states there has been some movement to offer legal protection to companies providing good-faith references, simply because it is not in the public interest to perpetuate the current situation. Nevertheless, threats of defamation, combined with the limited validity of reference checking, make this a less than ideal alternative to honesty testing under most circumstances. Background investigations on the other hand, with adequate legal safeguards, are a meaningful alternative if they are sufficiently comprehensive. Comprehensive investigations are, however, much more costly.

DRUG TESTING

As we use the term ''drug testing'' here, it applies to physiological procedures used to identify drug residuals in the body. Analyses of urine samples are widely used, although other procedures such as blood testing have some advantages. There has been considerable concern over legal strictures, especially as related to privacy issues, but still the law is more favorable to drug testing than opposed. There is a real legal concern regarding the safety implication of drug use in the workplace.

In practice a problem exists with regard to the accuracy of drug tests, primarily due to failures to establish the presence of drugs when they are in fact present. Yet extremely accurate procedures are available; they simply cost more. A study carried out in the U.S. Postal Service by Jacques Normand, Stephen Salyards, and John Mahoney and reported in the *Journal of Applied Psychology* (1990) indicated that:

The amount of lost productivity associated with hiring job applicants who test positive indicates that the U. S. Postal Service could save approximately $4,000,000 in undiscounted and unadjusted productivity costs in the first year, and that the accrued savings for one cohort of new employees over their tenure would be about $52,750,000. (p. 637)

Results such as these argue strongly for drug testing. As James Ledvinka and Vida Scarpello note in their book *Federal Regulation of Personnel and Human Resource Management* (1991), although federal law is favorable, state legislation can on occasion be restrictive; there is considerable variation from state to state. Furthermore, as Brian Heshizer and Jan Muczyk indicate in the *Labor Law Journal* (1987), the law is still evolving.

Clearly, in most jurisdictions drug testing for new hires is legal. Concerns about invasion of privacy plague many employers as well as applicants. Many people would like to find an alternative to the widely used urine tests. Impairment testing, which utilizes a computerized video test to obtain a measure of eye-hand coordination, shows promise. However, it is intended for the monitoring of current employees so as to maintain a safe working environment. It is not a screening procedure.

There can be no guarantee that pre-employment drug testing will pick up everyone who might subsequently exhibit drug problems on the job, but it does tend to identify enough such people to pay its way. Unfortunately, it is focused specifically on the drug problem, and only peripherally deals with other problems such as theft. Drug testing is an alternative to honesty testing, but only for a small part of honesty testing. Thus it is most useful when a company knows that drugs are its main challenge.

USING APPLICATION FORMS AND BIOGRAPHICAL DATA

Application forms and biographical sources are provided by candidates and deal with their past histories, and in some cases their feelings about past behavior and events. The information may come from a resumé that they submit, an application blank that they complete, or a biographical form that contains questions dealing with early life experiences, hobbies, social relations, and other aspects of the individual's prior history. At times these biographical data forms may incorporate questions that overlap with those contained in personality tests. There is not always a clear demarcation between honesty testing and the use of biographical data.

Two studies carried out in the Detroit area by Richard Rosenbaum and published in the *Journal of Applied Psychology* (1976) can be used to illustrate this approach. In each instance a group of employees discharged for admitted theft was compared with a group of employees who separated voluntarily and were recommended for rehire. Using this procedure, application blank items characterizing those who had engaged in theft were identified, and a scoring procedure for these items was established. Weights of 2 were given to items on which the difference between the two groups was large, and of 1 to those on which the differences were of a lesser order. There were many other items on the application blank where the difference was too small to be meaningful, and these were not used.

Those individuals who engaged in theft were characterized by the author as follows:

Mass merchandiser (cashiers only)	**Supermarket (cashiers, stock clerks, butchers, and others)**
Weight 150 or more. (+2)	Full-time work sought. (+2)
Detroit address. (+2)	Does not want relative contacted in case of emergency. (+2)
Two or more previous jobs. (+2)	Number of dependents, other than none. (+1)
Does not wear eyeglasses. (+2)	Not attending school. (+2)
	Not living with parents. (+1)
Application carelessly prepared. (+2)	Substandard appearance of application. (+2)
At present address less than 13 years. (+1)	No middle initial specified. (+2)
Weight less than 130 pounds. (+1)	Does not own an automobile. (+2)
	Applicant recently consulted a physician. (+2)
	New employee is black. (+2)

Note that there is very little overlap between the two lists; weighted application blank predictors tend to be quite specific to the particular situation. Because application blanks are almost universally used, this approach is quite unobtrusive. Furthermore, checks with new samples not used to identify items and establish weights indicate that the approach is effective. Yet as Kevin Murphy indicates in *Honesty in the Workplace* (1993), there are problems:

1. Weighted application blanks can be openly discriminatory, particularly if factors such as race, gender, or income are directly entered into the equation.
2. The weights may be unstable, especially if they were originally estimated in small samples.
3. This approach lacks face validity. In other words the relevance of many items on an application blank for predicting integrity is not always obvious . . . accepting decisions based on weighted application blanks may present substantial problems. (p. 136)

For a number of reasons, including the fact that they tend to invite lawsuits, openly discriminatory items should not be used. However, blanks can be constructed that do not present this problem, and the other problems can be handled as well. Yet this approach is not widely used. A recent survey by David Terpstra and Elizabeth Rozell published in *Personnel Psychology* (1993) found only a 17 percent usage rate for weighted application blanks of any kind—the lowest rate of any of the selection practices studied. Blanks specifically tailored as alternatives to honesty tests almost certainly represent a small proportion of the 17 percent. Clearly, the research required to select items and establish weights is a barrier, and there need to be enough instances of validated problem behaviors to justify the research. On the other hand, application blank data are readily available, and the approach does work. It is an acceptable alternative to honesty testing where appropriate studies can be carried out.

INTEGRITY INTERVIEWING

Training programs to teach skills in integrity interviewing are offered by a number of polygraph and honesty testing firms. Advertising materials used to promote the training illustrate the approach. The workshops conducted by one such firm are described as teaching:

How to reduce the risk of negligent hiring by identifying high-risk applicants.

How to use a practical three-step process to discuss sensitive topics and get honest answers.

How to overcome the seven behavioral attitudes of applicants who are likely to withhold information.

The two most important characteristics of the interview room setting.

What you can legally ask applicants and what questions may lead to discrimination.

How to read the applicant's verbal and non-verbal behavior.

How to establish company standards of acceptable behavior.

How to determine whether the applicant has falsified any information on the application blank or resumé.

Integrity interviews utilize both verbal responses to questions and behavioral cues of a non-verbal nature to reach conclusions regarding deception and dishonesty. Some interviewers use the approach like a stress interview, and the interrogation is not unlike a third degree. Others strive to put the candidate at ease and establish a close rapport, which might induce confessions. In some instances a highly structured procedure is followed, with standardized questions and a pre-established order. In other cases the strategy is to follow leads wherever they appear to emerge, and thus the interview is based in large part on hunch and intuition. A common approach is to use hypothetical scenarios and then ask what the candidate would do in such a situation. Questions about behavior in previous jobs, especially dishonest behavior, are frequently used.

In *Honesty in the Workplace* (1993), Murphy notes a number of behavioral cues that might be present in an interview, and that have been found at least to some degree to be associated with deception. Hesitation in speaking, higher pitch, and speech errors are verbal in nature. Non-verbal cues include increased blinking, frequent swallowing, fast or shallow breathing, rubbing or scratching, and masking smiles (not enjoyment smiles). In the *American Psychologist* (1991), Paul Ekman and Maureen O'Sullivan report studies indicating that some professionals, such as members of the U.S. Secret Service, can use these kinds of cues to detect deception successfully. Yet most people cannot.

Thus, the non-verbal side of integrity interviewing can be informative for those who know how to use it, but in most instances it adds little to what comes directly from the questioning. Obtaining confessions stands out as the ultimate objective. Generally highly structured employment interviews, with a preset protocol of questions, have been found to be superior to unstructured interviews, as Robert Dipboye indicates in his book *Selection Interviews: Process Perspectives* (1992). Yet nothing is known on this issue with regard to integrity interviews specifically.

Do integrity interviews have potential as alternatives to honesty testing? We think they do, but there is much still to be learned. The added input from behavioral cues, many of them of a non-verbal nature, could be beneficial. Honesty testing, computerized testing, and even computer interviews do not incorporate these cues, but they have the capacity for lower costs, simply because interviewers (and their time) are not needed. On the other hand, most companies interview anyway, and the added expense of an integrity component may be minimal. We view this as a promising, but as yet unproven, alternative. It seems likely that the skills of the interviewer will prove to be an important component of validity, however.

PERSONALITY TESTING AND ASSESSMENT

Let us start with graphology, the use of handwriting to infer personality characteristics. This is not a widely used approach in the U.S., but it does enjoy considerable popularity in Europe and in Israel. In its purest form it is concerned only with the writing itself, not its content. Gershon Ben-Shakhar and his colleagues present evidence that graphologists can make effective predictions of a job applicant's performance. Writing in the *Journal of Applied Psychology* (1986) they find, however, that these predictions are no better than those of nongraphologists examining the same material from a more clinical perspective. Simply put, it does not seem to be the nature of the handwriting that makes the real difference. But even more important for present purposes is the fact that graphology deals with personality generally, not with those aspects particularly germane to honesty testing. We know nothing about its capability in this latter regard. Yet evidence from many sources indicates that personality tests which focus on specific job-related issues, rather than "personality in general," do best in the employment domain. Graphology is not focused in this respect, and thus appears unsuitable as an alternative to honesty testing.

This matter of focus is important, because in the past personality tests have often been judged to be lacking in their capacity to predict job performance. However, the tests considered have measured personality characteristics important in clinical practice and the assessment of psychopathology, not employment. When modified to focus on specific kinds of employment screening, these tests have had a much better record.

Thus David McClelland and his colleagues, writing in *The Achievement Motive* (1953), and with David Winter in a book entitled *Motivating Economic Achievement* (1969), have shown how the Thematic Apperception Test (where stories are told using pictures as a stimulus) can be utilized effectively to focus on the performance of entrepreneurs. Similarly, Zygmunt Piotrowski and Milton Rock, in *The Perceptanalytic Executive Scale* (1963), demonstrate how the Rorschach Test (where the images created by ambiguous inkblots are described) can be scored to predict success among corporate executives. John Miner describes in his book *Role Motivation Theories* (1993) how sentence completion scales, normally used to diagnose emotional problems, may be adapted to predict effective performance in managers, professionals, and entrepreneurs (each with a different adaptation).

In all of these instances the personality measure is directly focused on some type of job, or aspect of performance. Accordingly, in order to predict honesty-related performance, it would seem that a personality test would need to focus on such matters, and not on ''personality in general.''

In the honesty area, personality-based (or personality-oriented or veiled-purpose) tests, take a set of more comprehensive and general personality items and cull them down to focus on honesty concerns. This would seem to be much more effective than using a larger number of items, many of which have no relation to honesty at all. It is like using a shotgun versus a rifle.

An approach to personality testing and assessment that has achieved considerable credence recently utilizes the so-called big five personality dimensions. A good discussion of this approach is contained in an article by Murray Barrick and Michael Mount in *Personnel Psychology* (1991). The five dimensions are extraversion, emotional stability, agreeableness, conscientiousness, and openness to experience. Of these, the only one focused directly on honesty is conscientiousness, which includes concepts related to dependability, thoroughness, and self-control, as well as being hard-working, persevering, careful, and organized. However, Deniz Ones, Chockalingam Viswesvaran, and Frank Schmidt note in the *American Psychologist* (1995) that the emotional stability and agreeableness factors have some relation to honesty as well.

Honesty tests of all types seem to tap into the conscientiousness dimension in one way or another; that is the conclusion reached by Ones, Viswesvaran, and Schmidt in their comprehensive review of the field in the *Journal of Applied Psychology* (1993). Thus using more broadly based personality tests as alternatives to honesty tests serves no real purpose. The net cast is likely to catch a large number of fish that only have to be thrown back, and probably fewer of those that one really wants to catch.

CONCLUSIONS

A number of alternatives to honesty testing do exist, although in each case qualifying considerations are involved. Polygraph testing can be useful, especially to the extent it induces confessions (if it is legally available). References can provide valuable information if accountability can be achieved, and the threat of defamation actions overcome. Background investigations represent a very attractive alternative if sufficiently comprehensive. Drug testing works well for its intended purpose if the need is great enough to justify it. Weighting application forms and biographical inventories are appropriate if the needed prior research can be, and is, carried out. Integrity interviewing offers a great deal of promise—if we only knew more about how to do it well.

Overall we are quite optimistic about these alternatives. However, we recognize that others may not share this optimism; you may want to consider the arguments set forth by John Jones in Chapter 3 of his book *Preemployment Honesty Testing* (1991) in this regard. We also believe that using several different approaches, rather than just one, is the preferred procedure. Thus honesty testing might be combined with a background investigation and a drug test, as well as an integrity interview. Or some other combination could be used. But we are getting ahead of ourselves. First we need to look into how well honesty tests work.

3

Do Honesty Tests Really
Measure Honesty?

We now need to present some technical concepts from the fields of psychology and statistics. Some readers will already be familiar with these concepts, and they can merely glance through the next section. Others, however, may lack this familiarity. If that is the case, our intention is to provide an opportunity to learn. The idea is to be sure that all readers are able to "start on the same page" as we approach the studies dealing with whether honesty tests do measure honesty.

These technical concepts involve the logic of research design for selection purposes and the conduct of statistical analyses. They are important for two reasons. First, you need to understand the studies that constitute the bulk of this chapter, and why the research was conducted as it was. Second, these psychological and statistical concepts influence the language that test publishers and their representatives use in talking and writing about their tests. One cannot evaluate a test without understanding what they are saying. Furthermore, it is our experience that on occasion representatives of test publishers misuse these concepts and reveal their own ignorance regarding their products. We do not believe this type of ignorance is widespread, but it is well to be able to recognize it where it exists.

THE LOGIC OF SELECTION (INCLUDING A STATISTICAL ASIDE)

The objective in selection is to identify and hire those individuals most likely to perform well on the job over a substantial period of time. To discover which selection procedures will accomplish this end, analyses should be carried out relating pre-employment or pre-placement data on candidates for a position to indexes of performance effectiveness. These measures of performance are typically called *criteria*. Evidence of theft, drug and alcohol use, production deviance, sabotage, and violence on the job can serve as criteria.

The logic of selection is best understood in the context of the *predictive validity* approach, which uses a series of steps as follows:

1. Decide on the selection procedures to be used—presumably including some type of honesty test.
2. Administer these selection procedures to a group of at least 30 candidates (preferably many more) who are subsequently hired for the job. Those hired should not be limited to those who score high or do best on the measures.
3. Collect criterion data on the post-hire performance of these individuals.
4. Establish the degree of relationship between the various selection measures and the performance criteria. This may be done in various ways, but the usual practice is to employ some type of statistical index such as a *correlation coefficient*. It may also be done by comparing the test performance of criterion groups—high versus low, good versus bad, honest versus dishonest, and so on.
5. Utilize the measure(s) with the greatest validity thus established in making future selection decisions.

When only a few selection measures are under study, this approach is sufficient. However, when the number of predictors considered rises above two or three, there is a real possibility that rather large correlation coefficients will begin to appear by chance alone, and thus the same predictive efficiency will not be present when the measures are put to use. To deal with this problem, the usual procedure is to resort to *cross validation*, which involves carrying out the validity study on another separate group to see if the same measures have high validity coefficients once again.

Predictive validity presents problems simply because it is time-consuming; one has to wait to gather the criterion data. Another approach to studying criterion-related validity, called *concurrent validity*, circumvents this difficulty by collecting predictor and criterion measures on current employees at essentially the same time. For a number of reasons, this approach will not work as well as predictive validation for identifying selection measures that will work in practice. Predictive validity certainly is to be preferred, but concurrent validity is better than no validation at all.

Obviously applying this approach involves the use of statistical analyses. Correlation coefficients must be calculated and a determination made as to whether they are large enough to be meaningful. Or average test scores in high and low groups must be compared to determine whether the difference between them is sufficiently large.

The final output in the conduct of a validity study is a distribution of test scores and of criterion scores. Such a distribution can be developed for each measure employed in the study. In the most common distribution in which the scores spread out over a range of values, there is a sizable concentration of scores near the middle with gradually declining frequencies on both sides of the distribution, to the point where at the high and low score extremes there may be only one person with a given value.

In instances such as this, one typically needs some kind of overall summary statistic to provide a general index of how well the subjects do. Usually this summary statistic is an average, or measure of central tendency. The most common procedure is to calculate a mean by totaling all the scores and dividing by the number of subjects.

A second measure used to describe distributions, in addition to a measure of central tendency, is a measure of the spread or variability of scores. One could use the range from the lowest to the highest score for this purpose, but the range is a very unstable measure in that it may change from one group of subjects to another with practically no change in the overall distribution.

The most commonly used measure of the spread of scores is the standard deviation (SD). A large SD means that the scores are widely spread around the mean; a small SD means that they are closely clustered.

In the case of the normal, bell-shaped score distribution which is approximated so frequently in validation research, 34 percent of all scores will fall between the mean and the score which is one standard deviation above it. Since this type of distribution is symmetrical, the same holds for the scores between one SD below the mean and the mean. Thus, 68 percent of the scores fall within plus or minus one SD from the mean. If one goes out another SD, proportionately fewer additional scores are picked up even though the score range is doubled, because the frequencies decline as one moves to the extremes. Thus, roughly 95 percent of the scores are between minus and plus two SDs, and well over 99 percent are between minus and plus three SDs.

Government enforcement agencies and current practice have characteristically specified the 0.05 level ($p < 0.05$) as the maximum significance acceptable for demonstrating validity. Below the 0.05 level the relationship is said to be *statistically significant* or reliable; above that level it is not. What does this mean?

The concept of significance level relates primarily to generalization. To what extent can one be certain that a relationship (such as that between test and criterion) found to exist in one sample of employees will also appear in other samples? This is an important consideration in validation research, because the value of the research depends on generalization of the results to new groups of candidates for the positions studied.

This potentiality for accurate generalization of a result is typically expressed in terms of the probability (p) that a relationship in the same direction as that found in the experimental sample will appear in successive samples drawn from the same population. Thus, a positive validity coefficient significant at the 0.05 level means that the chances of obtaining a sample correlation value that high or higher when the correlation in the whole population is, in fact, 0.00 are less than 5 in 100. Clearly, a 19-out-of-20 bet is a reasonably good one. On the other hand, if one is studying a large number of independent predictor-criterion relationships, chance alone will yield one "significant" relationship for every 20 studied. This is why cross-validation is so important in such multi-measure studies. It also points up the value of establishing even lower p values if possible—at the 0.01 level, for instance, where failures can be expected only one time in a hundred.

The significance of the various statistical measures can be calculated directly using the appropriate formulas. Many of the standard statistical computer programs do this automatically and provide a p value for each statistic. However, p values for most commonly used measures also may be obtained from tables presented in most statistics texts. If the value obtained in a study is above that tabled for the 0.05 level, the statistic is significant at $p < 0.05$; if it is in addition large enough to exceed the tabled value for the 0.01 level, it is significant at $p < 0.01$. Should the statistic's value be less than that required for the 0.05 level, it is generally considered not significant (n.s.).

Where it is feasible to compute means and where the data distributions approximate the normal form, with the larger frequencies in the middle and symmetrically smaller frequencies at the extremes, the t-test typically is used to compare the mean scores in two groups to see if the difference between the means is large enough to warrant a conclusion that the groups differ in a statistically significant manner. This type of analysis might be used, for instance, to evaluate the difference between the mean test scores of known problem and non-problem employees.

However, correlation coefficients are typically used to provide an index of the *degree* of relationship present. This measure of degree may then be tested, using available tables for the statistic to determine whether it is large enough to warrant the position that it is significantly different from 0. Thus, correlation procedures can provide a measure both of the size of test-criterion relationships and of their significance. It is also possible to determine through appropriate analyses whether one correlation coefficient is significantly different from another, not just different from 0. All of these considerations argue strongly for using correlational techniques in validation research wherever possible; it is the usual practice to do so.

Correlations may vary from -1.00 through 0 to $+1.00$. The larger values, both negative and positive, indicate a closer relationship, and thus are indicative of greater validity. Negative correlation coefficients indicate a tendency for high values in one distribution (test or criterion) to go with low values in the other. Positive coefficients indicate a tendency for high values in both distributions to go together (and low with low).

COMPARISONS WITH POLYGRAPH PERFORMANCE

With some knowledge of how validity studies are conducted we can now move to a discussion of actual research aimed at determining whether honesty tests do, in fact, measure and predict honesty and dishonesty. A number of different types of studies have been carried out for this purpose, and used by test publishers to champion their products. We will discuss each type and in each instance provide several examples. Thus, the reader should gain a knowledge not only of how valid the tests are, but of what to expect by way of honesty test validation research.

Because early honesty tests with a clear-purpose were initiated by security firms and companies involved in polygraph testing, it is not surprising that early validation research used the polygraph as a criterion. This approach was used in the studies published by Philip Ash in the *Journal of Applied Psychology* in 1971. Working at McKesson and Robbins, he identified approximately 250 applicants who had completed both an honesty test and the polygraph during the pre-employment evaluation. The correlation between the hiring recommendations from the two sources was 0.43, significant at $p < 0.01$. Both instruments elicited a large number of confessions, accounting for much of the relationship between the two. Ash notes "Incredible as it may seem, applicants in significant numbers do admit to practically every crime on the books" (p. 162).

In a much more recent study conducted by Michael Cunningham and published in the *Journal of Business and Psychology* (1989), 316 applicants for positions in 66 Chicago and northern Indiana businesses were given both a clear-purpose honesty test and a polygraph examination. However, in this instance only admissions during the polygraph interview were used to establish the employment recommendations. Thus, the criterion measure was based on confessions obtained with the assistance of the polygraph. The validity coefficient was 0.52, a correlation which was significantly different from zero at the 0.01 level.

In our own research we used polygraph results to select items for inclusion in the final clear-purpose honesty test. Thus, the test itself consisted of those items from a much larger pool which best discriminated between those who passed the polygraph and those who failed it. Similar approaches have been used in developing many of the overt honesty tests currently on the market. Table 3.1 gives the results we obtained in a group of 100 job applicants administered both the final honesty test and the polygraph. In some cases the honesty test came first, but just as often the polygraph was administered first; the order depended on the polygraphers' schedules.

Table 3.1 reflects the full range of polygraph results, not just those with scores at the extremes. The validity coefficient is 0.69, again highly significant. Note that although there are a few people who pass the polygraph with no problems whatsoever yet score below average on the honesty test, there are more cases where the honesty test appears not to identify the existence of dishonesty. Even with a rather high validity coefficient there are errors. Yet the overall result, as reflected in the Percent Honest column, certainly favors the use of this type of test.

Paul Sackett, writing with various co-authors, has published several reviews dealing with the relationship between honesty tests and the polygraph. Three of these reviews appeared in *Personnel Psychology* (1979, 1984, 1989) and one in

Table 3.1
Relationship between Honesty Test Score and Polygraph Results in a Group of
100 Job Applicants

| Honesty Test Score | Polygraph Results | | Percent Honest |
	Some Evidence of Dishonesty	No Evidence of Dishonesty	
65-69	0	2	
60-64	3	19	88
55-59	10	3	
50-54	13	8	32
45-49	13	0	
40-44	10	4	15
35-39	6	0	
30-34	5	0	0
25-29	3	0	
20-24	1	0	0

a book edited by John Bernardin and David Bownas (1985). Based on these reviews, and some additional data, the average validity coefficient appears to be in the high 0.50s, although there are figures in the 0.70s and even 0.80s. The higher values tend to be reported by test publishers in their own publications, not in the regular professional literature. Nevertheless, the overall picture from this source is very positive. This is a high level of validity for a psychological test. It appears to result in large part from confessions elicited by both measures.

COMPARISON WITH NON-POLYGRAPH CONFESSIONS

A study by Alan Frost and Fred Rafilson published in the *Journal of Business and Psychology* (1989) used an overt integrity test and a personality-based test in a validation study relating the tests to criteria involving theft and production deviance. The criteria were self reports obtained anonymously at the same time the tests were completed. The sample studied consisted of 105 already employed individuals from a wide range of occupations and firms. The personality-based measure did exhibit some validity in that it correlated 0.26 with production deviance, which was at $p < 0.01$. However, the overt integrity test yielded results which were of similar significance against the theft criterion at 0.46 and the production deviance criterion at 0.39. The two honesty tests were related, but only with a correlation of 0.25. Clearly in this instance the overt integrity test was more useful.

Another approach focuses on job applicants and asks them to complete both an honesty test and some type of measure of past criminal activity as a criterion. This approach was utilized in a study reported in Chapter 12 of John Jones's

Preemployment Honesty Testing (1991a). Some 104 applicants for jobs in convenience stores were studied. The honesty test scores dealing with drug activities produced a correlation with self-reported drug crimes of 0.45, and those focusing on theft correlated with self-reported theft crimes at 0.45 as well. The honesty test measure dealing with violence was not as effective (highest correlation 0.22). All of these correlations are significant at at least $p < 0.05$.

Surveys of the available research, such as those conducted by Paul Sackett, yield a wide range of validity coefficients using confession criteria. The overall pattern is one of statistical significance, with coefficients as high as 0.70 reported. However, the more likely result is something in the 0.40s. These validity coefficients tend to run lower than those for the polygraph. We think this is because both honesty test and polygraph-provoked confessions occur in a context where the subject fears that the examiner has some hidden means of finding out anyway. Where the criterion is merely simple admission, this is not the case, and the validity coefficients drop accordingly.

COMPARISON WITH PROBLEM BEHAVIOR ON THE JOB

Here we are concerned with studies that do not rely on confessions as criteria in any way, but rather utilize actual on-the-job behavior related to honesty. Probably the best study of this kind is reported by John Bernardin and Donna Cooke in the *Academy of Management Journal* (1993). It involved employees of a convenience store chain. The chain utilized an elaborate surveillance system that included videotapes, computer data, and undercover operatives to identify thieves on its payroll. Approximately half of the 111 employees studied were subsequently found to have engaged in theft of some kind. All of these individuals were terminated for cause and none appealed. The best estimate of validity was a correlation coefficient of 0.35 with $p < 0.01$. In this predictive validity design, the results indicated that the pre-employment honesty test worked to identify those subsequently caught stealing.

In contrast to the preceding study, which utilized an overt honesty test, Fred Rafilson, in the *Journal of Business and Psychology* (1988) reports on a validity study where the test was of a personality-based nature and contained no items that made direct reference to theft or honesty. This research is also distinguished by the fact that the criterion was broadly defined to include problem behavior extending well beyond theft. Applicants were tested prior to employment in a retail setting and all were hired regardless of test scores. Over a six-month period, 651 employees were considered successful in that no major problems arose. The remaining 585 employees did have problems, and were in fact fired— 329 for poor work performance, 172 for excessive absenteeism or tardiness, and 84 for violation of company rules and policies including those related to theft.

Among those who subsequently proved successful, 78 percent would have been accepted for employment by the test and 22 percent would have been rejected. Among the employees fired for poor performance, 37 percent would have been rejected; among those fired for absence and tardiness this figure was also 37 percent; among those fired for rule violations it was 47 percent. In all cases the rejection rate in the problem group was significantly ($p < 0.01$) greater than in the successful group. Thus, the test has the potential to do what it is supposed to do—get rid of problem employees.

Generally studies utilizing problem behavior on the job as the criterion yield validity coefficients in the high 0.20s and low 0.30s. This conclusion is based on several different research reviews. A problem is that many studies using the theft criterion end by detecting very little theft. Much theft simply goes undetected. In these studies, large numbers of people who do not steal and of undetected thieves are compared with very small numbers of detected thieves. This kind of situation tends to produce low validity coefficients which are in all likelihood underestimates. The solution is to use designs such as those employed by Bernardin and Cooke or Rafilson which do not introduce this imbalance. When this is done, validities in the 0.30s can be anticipated; this is still well below what is obtained using the polygraph and confessions, but certainly in line with the findings when other types of psychological measures (such as intelligence tests) are used.

COMPARISON OF CRIMINALS AND NON-CRIMINALS

This approach to validation has usually involved comparison of incarcerated criminals with a group of non-criminals such as job applicants. On occasion those found in a background investigation to have a criminal record are used in the comparison. The term "contrasted group design" is often used to refer to studies of this type.

An early report on this kind of research by Harrison Gough was published in *Personnel Psychology* (1971). Several groups of adult criminals and juveniles, all convicted of various crimes, were compared with a wide range of non-criminals, including high school students, college students, department store applicants, and office workers. A personality-based honesty test was used. In every instance the mean scores for the criminal groups differed substantially from those for the non-criminals. The validity coefficient using a non-criminal/criminal criterion was 0.58.

A more recent study utilized 329 federal prison inmates from 23 prisons who had been convicted of a wide range of white collar crimes. The most frequent crimes were bank fraud, bank embezzlement, internal revenue service fraud, currency counterfeiting, computer and wire fraud, forgery, and postal fraud. The comparison group consisted of 320 individuals in white collar positions of authority in banks, city governments, county government, and a state university. The authors of the study, Judith Collins and Frank Schmidt, writing in *Personnel Psychology* (1993), reported a correlation of 0.62 between a personality-based honesty test and the non-criminal/criminal criterion.

Figure 3.1
Prison and Normative Samples Compared

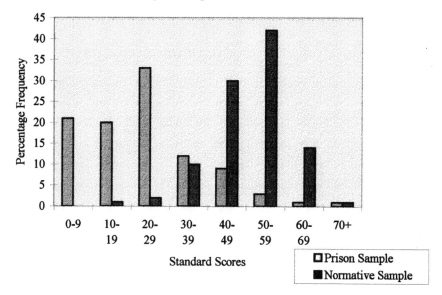

Both of the preceding studies were conducted with personality-based tests. We have conducted a similar study with an overt honesty test and published a report in *Polygraph* (1990). The criminals were 117 prisoners in five different institutions in Georgia. Within this group 91 percent were known property of-fenders (theft), 75 percent had alcohol and/or drug problems, and 14 percent had committed violent crimes. Comparisons were made with groups of job ap-plicants. Whereas these non-criminals had a mean test score of 50, the criminals scored only 22. Utilizing a t-test, a significant difference at the 0.01 level was found. In completing the honesty test, 97 percent of the criminals confessed to one or more crimes; only 11 percent of the non-criminals did the same. Figure 3.1 depicts the difference in score distributions between the two groups.

Clearly this type of contrasted group study produces substantial differences, with coefficients in the high 0.50s and 0.60s. Given the extreme nature of the criminal groups, this is not surprising. There has, in fact, been some contention that studies of this kind should not be used as evidence of honesty test validity because the criminals are so extreme that they do not represent the type of person likely to be found among job applicants. Yet it is also true that if large validity coefficients were not found, that fact would almost certainly be used as evidence of the invalidity of honesty tests. Overall we conclude that studies using crim-inals in a contrasted group design do make a contribution to the understanding of honesty test validity. They are a useful addition to the portfolio of validation approaches.

COMPARISONS AGAINST INVENTORY SHRINKAGE

These are studies that use inventory shrinkage (presumably as a result of theft) as a criterion. A study reported by Scott Martin and Loren Lehnen and published in *Personnel Journal* (1992) defined shrinkage as the difference between actual inventory and what the inventory should be if there were no pilferage, misclassifications, breakage, and clerical errors. For retailers, such as the department store company studied, internal theft is likely to account for some 30 to 40 percent of these shortages.

The company initially had a shrinkage rate across its 30 stores of 2.8 percent of sales. Subsequently an honesty testing program for new hires was implemented in an effort to reduce that figure. The test was of the clear-purpose variety; with it in place the annual shrinkage rate dropped to 1.9 percent. This presumably occurred both because dishonest employees were screened out, and because the existence of the testing program sent a message to current employees, thus changing the honesty climate. After two years of testing there was a major management change in the company, and the testing program was eliminated. In the ensuing year the shrinkage figure rose to a surprising 4.1 percent.

Most inventory shrinkage studies use only the pretest and testing periods, not the reversal aspect. They tend to find reduced shrinkage with the implementation of testing, but it is entirely possible that something other than the honesty testing program caused this. The ideal study would include other locations that did not undergo honesty testing, but which were otherwise comparable to those that did. The Martin and Lehnen study is to be preferred because it includes the reversal period, but even better would be a study that included a parallel non-test component. We know of no such study.

Another approach is to take locations with a high incidence of shrinkage (bad security) and compare them with low incidence locations (good security) in terms of mean honesty test scores. We were involved in such a study in a drugstore chain where 9 bad-security and 12 good-security stores were compared. A problem arose in that solid shrinkage figures were not available for all locations, and thus the opinion of the security manager had to be substituted. Comparisons between individuals from the two types of locations yielded a significant difference ($p < 0.01$) on 18 honesty test questions. However, these items represented only 13 percent of the total questionnaire. Other analyses suggested that only as few as 8 percent of the items in the total questionnaire should have been considered significant, and half of these were not, in fact, contained in the final test (this study was carried out before the final comparisons with polygraph results were completed).

We conclude that shrinkage studies are difficult to conduct, and even more difficult to conduct well. There are problems in documenting shrinkage, knowing how much shrinkage is related to employee theft, and in making attributions to theft as opposed to other causes. The study in which we were involved was certainly flawed in several respects, and we are not sure that others can overcome all of these difficulties. Nevertheless, where validity coefficients are calculated, and that is not often, the figures can be quite acceptable. In fact, correlations between shrinkage rates in various locations and average honesty test scores as high as -0.55 have been reported.

COMPARISONS AGAINST OVERALL JOB PERFORMANCE

Studies in which honesty test scores are compared with ratings or other measures of overall job performance are in many respects problematic. If the job is one in which opportunities for problem behavior, such as theft, are high, then some level of validity would be expected. On the other hand, there are many cases where honesty problems would represent a major negative if they became evident, but until they do, which is rare, they simply do not enter into the overall evaluation process. This appeared to be the case in a study involving Assistant Store Managers reported by Jeffrey Berman in the *Journal of Business and Psychology* (1993). Yet the more common pattern is a correlation in the low 0.20s, which is statistically significant. Such findings have been reported for a personality-based measure by Joyce and Robert Hogan in the *Journal of Applied Psychology* (1989). Similar results were obtained in studies reported by Fred Rafilson in the *Journal of Business and Psychology* (1988). Apparently, overt and personality-based measures do about equally well.

In general, honesty tests should be validated against honesty criteria. If more comprehensive performance criteria are used, validities would be expected to correspond to the extent to which honesty considerations enter into the work. Normally, however, one would not expect validity coefficients involving overall job performance to equal those obtained with more honesty-focused criteria such as polygraph results, confessions, or criminal behavior. From what we can determine, they usually do not.

COMPARISONS WITH OTHER TESTS

A final approach to the validation of honesty tests, which has been recommended on occasion, involves administering the honesty test and some other test to a group of people, and calculating the correlation between the two measures. In essence the other test becomes the criterion in the validation study.

Research reported by Philip Ash in the *Journal of Business and Psychology* (1991c) provides an example of how this procedure may be used. An experimental honesty test containing both overt integrity and personality-based items, many of which focused on early childhood experiences, had received very little validation, and none in the business context. In order to look into its validity, it was compared with another test of the overt variety which had been studied extensively using a number of the validity designs described in this chapter. Both tests were administered to 225 applicants for clerical and warehouse jobs in a national drug distribution company as part of the standard selection process.

A correlation of 0.56 ($p < 0.01$) was obtained between the two tests, suggesting that the experimental test held considerable promise.

Here the criterion test was a well-validated measure of the honesty type. A similar approach has been used on occasion where the criterion employed is a general personality test which, although known to be useful for clinical diagnosis and vocational counseling, has not been specifically validated in the honesty context. Studies of this kind can help gain an understanding of the honesty construct, but they should not be used as validation evidence for or against a test designed to screen out dishonest people from employment.

Usually in these cases it is assumed that the honesty test should exhibit certain relationships to specific scores derived from the general personality test. If it does the honesty test is valid; if not, it is invalid. The problem is that there is no pre-existing body of evidence validating the personality test scores as measures of honesty. An example reported by Robert Moore in the *Journal of Managerial Psychology* (1988) involved administering an honesty test and the Sixteen Personality Factor Questionnaire, or 16PF (a general personality test) to 96 college students in a classroom context. When the hypothesized relationships did not appear, the author concluded that the honesty test lacked validity. But there was no good reason to believe that the particular 16PF measures were indicative of honesty in the first place.

CONCLUSIONS

The studies described here typically have been published in respectable professional sources which require reviews by independent and knowledgeable individuals. They are part of the professional literature, not merely self-serving promotion pieces. In addition, we have described our own studies, many of which worked well, and one of which did not. We have reasonably good confidence in these results because we know what happened, and again we have nothing to sell.

The overall picture that emerges is quite positive. Honesty tests, using currently available designs, do exhibit good evidence of validity. Future research may unearth new designs for validation, but there is no reason to believe that these will yield different results. Yet when one looks at the reviews of the validation research extending back over the past 10 years, the conclusions are not nearly so positive. These reviews typically use both published and unpublished studies, with the latter usually being provided by test publishers. Perhaps the use of published results contributes to a more positive evaluation, because studies that fail to produce significant findings are rarely published. Yet one would expect that if there were any bias from the test publisher sources, it too would be of a distinctly positive nature. Of the eight major reviews that have been conducted to date, five are positive and three negative—not an overwhelming vote of confidence. Have we missed something, or do the negative votes reflect some hidden agendas? We consider this whole issue in the next chapter.

4

The Storm of Controversy: Validity as Assessed by Reviewers

We have indicated our own assessment of the validity of honesty tests. Some reviewers agree with us; some do not. Of the eight reviews that follow, two are particularly significant. They were widely awaited by potential purchasers of honesty tests, because they appeared to indicate the direction federal legislation would take. As the market awaited these decisions, it often failed to act at all, with the result that test sales leveled off, or even declined for a period.

These reviews were one conducted by the Office of Technology Assessment in 1990, and the other was sponsored and published by the American Psychological Association (APA) in 1991. The latter was authored by Lewis Goldberg (as chair), Julia Grenier, Robert Guion, Lee Sechrest, and Hilda Wing. Earlier, these two sources had combined to sound the virtual death knell of polygraph testing. Would they do so once again, to produce the same result for honesty tests? Many held their breath and did not buy, awaiting a decision. In the end it was a split verdict, and at least for the moment honesty testing did not go the way of the polygraph. Yet, as dramatic as was the situation created by these two reviews, other published reviews have exerted a substantial influence as well. Thus, we need to take a dispassionate look at the total picture. In doing so, we face directly the storm of controversy, and often the conflicting values, that have surrounded the honesty testing arena.

MCDANIEL AND JONES—1988 (POSITIVE)

Although we focus on the 1988 review by Michael McDaniel and John Jones published in the *Journal of Business and Psychology*, a less comprehensive review by the same authors was published in the same journal in 1986. Also, an abbreviated version of the 1988 article constitutes Chapter 8 of John Jones's book *Preemployment Honesty Testing* (1991a). All three of these reviews utilize a quantitative method of combining data from various sources to yield an overall validity coefficient.

This method, known as meta-analysis, is based on the idea that much of the variation in findings from one study to another is due to statistical and methodological artifacts, not real differences in underlying relationships. When appropriate corrections are applied to the data of individual studies, the approach yields an indication of whether there are real differences from one study to another, and of the true average correlation between test and criteria. The net effect is to determine if the validity results obtained legitimately can be generalized to new, but similar, situations in which no actual validation research has been carried out. In the process, an estimate of the average validity coefficient operating in the practical selection situation is obtained.

In the 1986 report this procedure was applied to data from seven studies utilizing a single testing instrument and criteria of dishonesty represented by supervisory ratings, polygraph measures, or self-reports. None of the seven studies had been published in the professional literature at the time. The findings indicated that generalization to non-validation settings was warranted, with validity coefficients as high as the low 0.50s. However, the number of studies on which these conclusions are based is so small that by today's standards this article would not be published in a recognized journal. Thus, this mini-review must be considered suggestive at best.

To their credit, the authors recognized this shortcoming and two years later published the results of a more comprehensive meta-analysis, again involving a single overt honesty test and various theft criteria. There were now 23 separate samples studied (reported in 17 sources). Most of the data came from unpublished technical reports and papers presented at professional conventions, but roughly a third of the studies had been formally published.

The conclusions from the 1986 meta-analysis were essentially replicated, now with an average validity in the low 0.50s and good support for validity generalization. The authors summarize their findings as follows:

The results from these meta-analyses indicate that the validity of the dishonesty scale is at useful levels regardless of the circumstances of its use. However, the measure achieves its highest validity when the subjects' responses are anonymous, when the criterion is a self-report measure, when the subjects are students, and when the respondent is aware that the investigator has another source of information on the subject's honesty. (pp. 337–338)

One could argue with the exclusion from the meta-analysis of certain additional studies noted in the article, with the fact that only a single test measure was used, with the degree to which increasing test sales may have motivated the analysis, and again with the still relatively small number of studies involved. Yet the results of the McDaniel and Jones reviews speak very positively for overt integrity testing to predict theft. They are also important because they report the first published meta-analyses in the field.

SACKETT AND COLLEAGUES—1989 (POSITIVE)

Chapters published in the *Annual Review of Psychology* are generally acknowledged to represent the essence of mainstream psychological science. They are up-to-date and prepared with close attention to both detail and comprehensiveness. In the 1992 chapter on personnel selection, Frank Schmidt, Deniz Ones, and John Hunter say "An excellent current source of research information on integrity tests is the review by Sackett et al. (1989)." This endorsement has been echoed elsewhere as well.

This review (et al. above refers to colleagues Laura Burris and Christine Callahan) had its roots in an article by Paul Sackett and Phillip Decker in *Personnel Psychology* in 1979. However, that article is clearly outdated today. Then, in 1984 Sackett and Michael Harris provided a more comprehensive review, again in *Personnel Psychology*, but with an expanded treatment in the edited volume *Personality Assessment in Organizations* (1985). In 1989 the 1984 material was updated to cover the intervening five years, again in *Personnel Psychology*. Thus, the articles subsequent to 1979 cover the literature through almost all of the 1980s. A more recent article by Sackett in *Current Directions in Psychological Science* (1994) is more of a commentary than a review.

These reviews made extensive use of information provided by test publishers in various technical reports, in addition to studies in the published literature. Through the mid-1980s, 14 studies using the polygraph as a criterion were found, and three more were added by the end of the decade. In contrast, studies involving the use of external criteria such as terminations for theft and supervisory ratings increased dramatically from 1984 to 1989—from 7 to 31. Furthermore, studies of this type were often considered flawed in one way or another in the 1984 review, but the 24 new studies were considered as a group to be better conducted. Confessions were employed as criteria in 16 studies in the 1984 review. To this, six studies were added in 1989. While only one study reporting on inventory shrinkage was noted in 1984, there were three more by the end of the decade. Comparisons of criminals and non-criminals also increased from three in 1984, with the addition of two more studies.

Initially (in 1984) the reviewers noted the many substantial validity coefficients, but they were unwilling to take a firm position and state an overall conclusion. They reviewed the arguments pro and con, but did not endorse either position, while pushing for the conduct of more and better research. It was apparent from the later review, however, that much research of this kind now had occurred. Sackett and his colleagues indicate that criterion-related validity studies with external criteria are the most persuasive and that at the time of the initial review few of these existed. By 1989 they said:

The present review found a large number of studies using such a strategy, including large-scale predictive studies in which a substantial number of employees were dismissed for theft on the job and studies using a broad range of criteria, including absence, turnover, and supervisory ratings. Thus a more compelling case that integrity tests predict a number of outcomes of interest to organizations can be made today than at the time of the earlier review. (p. 520)

In his 1994 commentary, Sackett says:

A large body of validity evidence consistently shows scores on integrity tests to be positively related to both a range of counterproductive behaviors and supervisory ratings of overall performance. However, virtually all the research has been done by test publishers, leading skeptics to question whether only successes are publicized. (p. 74)

Although his caveat needs further discussion, Sackett clearly does not accept this view as his own. Over the years he has moved from a neutral position to a distinctly positive one, as the research base has continued to build.

O'BANNON, GOLDINGER, AND APPLEBY—1989 (POSITIVE)

While the preceding reviews were carried out by psychologists and published in the psychological literature, the contribution of Michael O'Bannon, Linda Goldinger, and Gavin Appleby is a joint effort by a psychologist, a human resource consultant, and a lawyer. It was published in a 226-page book. A very extensive effort was made to obtain validity information directly from test publishers. A Directory of Honesty Tests contained in the book lists 42 instruments. Of these, 33 are known to have been the subject of some research—almost 80 percent. In the great majority of these instances the research dealt with validity issues.

The review of validities did not include studies utilizing overall job performance, job tenure, or the polygraph as criteria; nor did it include correlations with other tests. Reports "which were ambiguous, incomplete, or not detailed enough to be properly evaluated" were excluded. The authors comment that "Studies in honesty testing appear to be guilty of such deficiencies more often than most areas of test research" (p. 70). Because of the extensive use of data obtained from test publishers and the way in which studies were selected for inclusion, this review appears to have covered somewhat different ground than the Sackett review, even though both appeared in the same year.

Studies using a contrasted group design (in most cases criminals and noncriminals) are noted for seven tests. In all instances the results are viewed as providing positive evidence for validity.

There were three tests that had been studied in relation to background checks on past criminal behavior. In all three instances, statistically significant relationships between test and criterion were reported.

Seven tests had been validated against a confession criterion, in several instances with multiple studies. All seven tests provided some statistically significant evidence for validity. However, there were specific studies where confessions were too few to warrant any conclusions.

Another category of validity studies used predictive designs with test scores compared against subsequent evidence of theft, cash shortages, and other types of dishonesty. Six tests were evaluated in this manner. Of these, half yielded evidence of significant validity. In the remaining cases the data provided, although suggestive, were insufficient to clearly establish validity. Low rates of dishonesty detection, well below what would have been believed to actually exist, represent a major problem.

A final type of study used measurements over time, usually in terms of inventory shrinkages when honesty tests were and were not in use. Four tests were assessed in this manner, and of these three proved valid in at least one of the studies conducted. In the other instance the results were considered uninterpretable.

O'Bannon, Goldinger, and Appleby do not provide an overall statement of their conclusions. However, although their analyses indicate a number of difficulties in the research and a need for more refined studies, the sum total of their reports on individual investigations using the various designs was distinctly positive. On balance one would have to conclude that these reports range from neutral to highly positive, depending on the study, with an average well into the positive range.

OFFICE OF TECHNOLOGY ASSESSMENT—1990 (NEGATIVE)

This is where the controversy begins. On September 25, 1990, the Office of Technology Assessment (OTA) released its final report on its two-year study of honesty tests, and that same day OTA testified before the House Subcommittee on Employment Opportunities. As documented by Wayne Camara in a report in *The Industrial-Organizational Psychologist* (1991), the American Psychological Association (APA) submitted testimony for the record at that hearing raising questions regarding the OTA findings. Representative Mathew Martinez (Democrat—California), as chair of the subcommittee, invited APA to present its full findings to that body when they became available.

The OTA was created in 1972 as an analytical arm of Congress. Its stated function is to help legislative policymakers anticipate and plan for the consequences of technological changes and to examine the many ways, expected and unexpected, in which technology affects people's lives. At the time of the report the congressional board overseeing the OTA was chaired by Senator Edward Kennedy (Democrat—Massachusetts). There is little doubt that the report was intended as a first foray in a battle to make honesty testing illegal at the federal level, in the same way that the polygraph had previously been proscribed.

A letter written by John Miner on October 31, 1990, to the marketing director of the company with which we then worked may help to explain what happened. The following excerpt represents an introduction, with the letter then going on to consider the relevance of the report for users of the specific test with which we were involved:

The report was written by an OTA Project Staff with direct assistance from five contractors. There are also 15 individuals who participated in an OTA workshop on integrity testing and 14 other reviewers and contributors who provided assistance in some form. With regard to these 29 contributors the report says "OTA assumes full responsibility for the report and the accuracy of its contents. Those who assisted OTA do not necessarily approve, disapprove, or endorse this report." Thus the report appears to be the product of the OTA Project Staff and the contractors. None of the OTA staff are psychologists. Three of the five contractors are members of the American Psychological Association. However, only one is a widely recognized and published industrial/organizational psychologist. That individual is also a member of the American Psychological Association Task Force on the Prediction of Dishonesty and Theft in Employment Settings, a group which appears to have reached conclusions on integrity testing that are in many respects just the opposite of those reached by OTA.

I point all this out because it raises questions in my mind about the legitimacy of the OTA report. Those responsible for the report are not outstandingly qualified for the purpose at hand. The only one among them whose qualifications are unquestionable seems to be in a position of endorsing two antithetical positions at the same time. Although I am sure he will subsequently provide an explanation of this situation, it is rather confusing at present. In any event, the OTA report is clearly not the product of well-known, widely recognized psychologists that the American Psychological Association effort is. The OTA report does not have the kind of highly qualified professional expertise behind it that one might hope for with an effort of this kind. At times this lack of expertise becomes clearly manifest in the report itself.

Another point that needs to be recognized up front is that while the report focuses directly and in considerable detail on the negative effects of integrity testing, it does not evaluate the benefits to employers, individuals, and society in the same manner (see p. 63 of the report). In short no attempt is made to provide a balanced assessment of the pros and cons of integrity testing. This focus on the negative is disturbing. Nevertheless, what is truly important is that it once again raises questions regarding the legitimacy of the whole effort.

Lest readers question the objectivity of this assessment at a time when we clearly did have some personal involvement with the field, we quote from the *Annual Review of Psychology* chapter by Frank Schmidt, Deniz Ones, and John Hunter (1992)—"The (OTA) study is superficial and in part clearly erroneous, but its tone is neutral to only mildly critical" (p. 641). We would add, however, that in comparison to existing reviews already in the literature "mildly critical" stands out in sharp contrast.

What, then, did the report conclude and how did its authors reach those conclusions? The stated methodology was as follows:

1. OTA studied the two most current reviews of the integrity testing literature (the Sackett, Burris, and Callahan and the O'Bannon, Goldinger, and Appleby reviews, both published in 1989), as well as reviews of individual tests published in major test review compendiums.
2. OTA reviewed copies of tests provided by leading publishers.
3. OTA reviewed studies conducted by major integrity test companies using detected theft and counterproductivity as criteria.
4. OTA conducted interviews with a number of experts on various aspects of testing.
5. As in any OTA report, comments were solicited from a wide range of reviewers on various aspects of the study, and on various drafts of the document. (p. 7)

Two findings are stated in the report:

1. The research on integrity tests has not yet produced data that clearly supports or dismisses the assertion that these tests can predict dishonest behavior. Given the paucity of independent confirmation of research results, problems identified in published reviews and in OTA's review of a sample of validity studies, and unresolved problems relating to the definition and measurement of the underlying psychological constructs, OTA finds that the existing research is insufficient as a basis for supporting the assertion that these tests can reliably predict dishonest behavior in the workplace.
2. Errors in test results, potential discriminatory impact, and potential violations of privacy raise important public policy issues pertaining to the use of integrity tests. (pp. 9–10)

Our concern in this chapter is with validity issues; thus, aspects of the second finding will have to await discussions in later chapters. However, it is important to note that the report ends with the sentence, "OTA believes that the potentially harmful effects of systematic misclassification, possible impacts on protected groups, and privacy implications of integrity tests combine to warrant further governmental attention." Presumably this is why OTA moved immediately to testimony before Congress.

With regard to the reviews noted previously in this chapter, which did not include the meta-analyses of McDaniel and Jones, the OTA report had this to say: "Although these reviews have been conducted by individuals who are generally sympathetic with the objectives of psychological and personnel testing, their findings are couched in cautious tones and their principal conclusion is that better research is very much needed."

We believe that what is happening here is a complete misunderstanding of the differences between scientific and managerial cultures, and their values. To explain what we mean, we draw upon statements originally set forth in a book by John Miner entitled *The Management Process.*

Caution and skepticism are characteristic of science. A scientist remains neutral until a convincing body of evidence is accumulated. This is a major aspect of scientific objectivity. Hunch and bias provide no basis for decisions; only controlled research and substantiated theory will do. "I don't know" thus becomes not only an acceptable answer to a question, but in many cases a highly valued one. By admitting that adequate knowledge to solve a problem or to make a decision is lacking, science opens the matter to research. From a scientific viewpoint the greatest error is that which occurs when inadequate or insufficient data are overinterpreted or overgeneralized, so that an unsolved problem is accepted as solved. Errors of this kind block scientific progress, because the identification of problems is made extremely difficult.

Managers, on the other hand, most often make decisions with insufficient or inadequate data. Unlike the scientist, managers are frequently faced with problems that cannot be answered with "I don't know." Often they must accumulate as much information as possible in the time available and then act. Such decisions may have a large element of risk, but when judgment cannot be deferred there is no alternative.

The difference between these two decision-making modes is substantial, and has resulted in considerable misunderstanding and mutual criticism. The role of the scientist requires recognition of what is known and what is not known in order to state problems for research. Scientists must take every precaution to ensure that their findings, once obtained, are not in error. In contrast, the managerial role does not require the advancement of knowledge but rather the achievement of organizational goals. Time is often a crucial factor in decision making. Risk and uncertainty are everywhere; although they should be recognized and not made an excuse for sloppy thinking, they cannot be avoided. In many cases the process of extended study—which is so essential to the scientist, and at the same time frequently so irritating to the manager when he or she seeks scientific assistance—simply is not possible. (pp. 70–71)

It appears that OTA has taken the caution inherent in scientific decision making, where it has functional value, and applied it to managerial decision making where it has no such value. The reviews indeed are saying that for scientific purposes "better research is needed," but they are also saying that for managerial purposes the evidence is sufficient to justify action. Whether OTA's failure to reflect this cultural differential was intended, or a consequence of insufficient scientific background and training, we cannot say. Nevertheless, it is an important factor that needs to be considered in interpreting the OTA report.

AMERICAN PSYCHOLOGICAL ASSOCIATION—1991 (POSITIVE)

We were not involved in the OTA review in any manner, other than the fact that our test is noted along with others in several footnotes. Our input to the American Psychological Association review was much more extensive, although we have no idea as to how influential it may have been.

The APA was instrumental in the passage of the Polygraph Protection Act. It is our impression that its officers came out of that experience with a generally negative view of any instrument designed to measure honesty for selection purposes. Thus, one officer of the organization is quoted in the February 6, 1989 issue of *Newsday* as indicating that he is "concerned about the validity of these (honesty) tests. We're hearing numerous claims of companies simply marketing polygraph questions on paper.''

Yet it is our impression that the APA study was much more open and wide-ranging than that of the OTA. We attribute this to the efforts of the task force members themselves—Lewis Goldberg as chairman, Julia Grenier, Robert Guion, Lee Sechrest, and Hilda Wing. They listened, and they appear to have rendered an objective judgment in the face of what was initially at least a rather negative context. An article by Tori DeAngelis in the *APA Monitor* (1991), which appeared subsequent to the publication of the APA report, seems to give some support to our view that in contrast to the OTA report, the APA report made better and more comprehensive use of scientific information. Through literature searches and previous reviews, more than 300 documents were obtained for the study, in addition to materials provided by test publishers.

Based on these analyses, the APA task force came to a set of conclusions at the end of its report. Those relating to validity are as follows:

The Task Force began its work with no strong presuppositions about paper-and-pencil measures of honesty and integrity, except perhaps for some skepticism about the likely evidence for their validity. We did, however, begin with the position that honesty tests should be judged by the same standards as other measures developed and used by psychologists.

We found that publishers of honesty tests are highly variable in the ways that they describe their tests, in the ways that they document them, and in the evidence that they assemble to substantiate claims of their validity and utility. For some published measures, almost no evidence at all is available beyond assurances that evidence exists. For a few measures, extensive research has been completed. However, even in the latter cases test publishers have relied on the cloak of proprietary interest to withhold information concerning the development and scoring of the tests, along with other basic psychometric information. The entire field of honesty testing would benefit greatly from substantially increased openness.

Published reviews of honesty tests, supplemented by our own analyses of the available literature, suggest that for those few tests for which validity information is available the preponderance of the evidence is supportive of their predictive validity. Assessment of their construct validity is hampered by inadequate formulation of the constructs presumed to underlie test performance. Nonetheless, to the extent that evidence is available, it is consistent with the idea that these tests reflect aspects of personal integrity and dependability, or trustworthiness.

Many test publishers have not come close to meeting standards for the publication, sale, and use of psychological measures, and these deficiencies should be promptly corrected. Many of these tests lack critical documentation of their psychometric properties, and we strongly urge employers *not* to use such tests. Despite all of our reservations about honesty tests, however, we do not believe that there is any sound basis for prohibiting their development and use; indeed, to do so would only invite alternative forms of pre-employment screening that would be less open, scientific, and controllable. (pp. 25–26)

Several points here bear comment. We agree that honesty tests should be judged by the same standards as any other tests. This is important because some people have on occasion put forth superstandards for honesty tests, calling for validity coefficients approximating 1.00 when correlations of the order of 0.30 or 0.40 are regularly accepted as evidence of validity outside the honesty testing context.

We also agree that much of the validity research has been done by a few test publishers, who incidentally have been in the market for some time and who tend to have a large share of that market. We strongly suspect that market share gives one the wherewithall to conduct research, and that evidence of validity obtained through research fuels further growth in market share. It should be noted, however, that within the two categories of overt integrity tests and personality-based measures, the items used in different tests tend to be very similar. This does not excuse a publisher from the need to demonstrate validity, but it does suggest that the validities that have been shown should generalize to other honesty tests as well.

Finally, the task force's recommendation against legislative strictures on honesty tests appears at least for now to have held back the momentum that began to build with the release of the OTA report. Although federal laws that impinge upon honesty testing in one way or another have been passed, there is nothing comparable to the Polygraph Protection Act.

An article by Wayne Camara and Dianne Schneider in the *American Psychologist* (1994) provides background on the APA review, and synthesizes its conclusions relative to those of the OTA.

GUASTELLO AND RIEKE—1991 (NEGATIVE)

This review, conducted by Stephen Guastello and Mark Rieke, is selective in that it deals with only three honesty tests. It excludes validation studies using the polygraph as a criterion and those making comparisons involving convicted criminals. In general the intent was to focus on theft criteria, and consequently the use of honesty tests to predict a broader range of criteria is not considered.

The flavor of the review, which appeared in *Behavioral Sciences and the Law* (1991), is best understood by cutting directly to its conclusions:

1. There is no support in psychological theory or research for the honesty construct as measured by honesty tests.

2. The tests are fakable.

3. The often-reported association between theft attitudes and theft has little or no external validity to actual behavior.

4. While the weighted average correlation between theft attitudes and theft behavior is statistically significant, theft attitudes account for less than 1 percent of the criterion variance, which is trivial.

5. Concomitantly, the utility of such tests is also trivial given the operational selection ratios and base rates of success.

6. The false accusations of theft exceed the Murphy criteria for establishing reasonable doubt with regard to the applicant's criminal behavior.

7. Issues of bias need to be resolved as they might pertain to college-educated applicants, the poorest sector of the working class, and religious beliefs.

The authors conclude that "honesty testing should be replaced by a more traditional selection strategy of positive proof, whereby applicants are selected on bona fide, positively defined, job requirements rather than screened out with confused and value-laden definitions of dishonesty" (pp. 515–516).

Do these conclusions follow from the analyses and arguments presented? The approach taken was to reanalyze existing studies using statistical approaches the reviewers considered to be more appropriate to the data. One such approach involves correcting validity coefficients to remove the effects of responding in a socially desirable manner (faking good). This procedure has not generally been used in honesty test research, but it is not unheard of. Previous use suggests only a negligible reduction in validity coefficients. Guastello and Rieke report average reductions of 0.12, 0.06, and 0.17 for the three tests they considered. Using this technique, the validity coefficient would be expected to decrease less than .10 in these studies. The impact is not sufficient to render the tests invalid.

Out of curiosity we applied this approach to our own data. We found no reduction whatsoever in the correlation of 0.69 between the honesty test and polygraph results. This was because responding in a socially desirable manner, and thus presumably faking good, was not related either to honesty test score or to the polygraph. Faking simply was not a meaningful issue. Given that honesty tests clearly can be constructed to avoid social desirability bias, that the effects in any event are not large, and that the approach taken in the review would be considered inappropriate by many psychologists, we are not persuaded by this line of argument.

The reviewers tend to look at honesty testing from the viewpoint of applicants who may be disadvantaged, rather than from that of an employer. The fact that there may be a number of false positives, where some honest people are rejected for employment along with the dishonest, is of this nature. False positives occur with all psychological testing, and in fact all selection procedures. To give the matter special consideration in the case of honesty tests is to apply superstandards to those tests only.

The review presents evidence that on one of the three tests college students scored *lower* than job applicants, suggesting bias against educated persons. This could well be due to the fact that the college students had little to lose, and did not take the test seriously. Table 4.1 presents our findings on this subject when all the individuals considered were tested as job applicants. There is clearly no evidence of a consistent bias against the college educated. Nor have other investigators reported such a phenomenon.

Table 4.1
Relationship between Honesty Test Scores and Educational Level Attained

	Mean Test Scores for Educational Groups					
	Some High School	High School Graduation	Some College	College Graduation	Significance of Group Comparisons	Correlation Between Test Score and Education
114 Black Women	39	38	40	39	None	0.05
116 Black Men	49	48	41	47	$p<0.01$	-0.17
168 White Women	35	38	38	39	None	0.15
202 White Men	45	43	42	43	None	-0.09

Note: The only statistically significant finding is the relatively low mean test score of the black men who attended, but did not graduate, from college. Comparisons should not be made across the four race and sex groups since each was scored on a separate scale designed to maximize validity for that group.

We do believe that selection should be based on job requirements (not "confused and value-laden definitions of dishonesty"). Others in the field, including David Arnold, John Jones, and William Harris writing in *Security Management* (1990) have taken this same position. Job analyses need to be conducted to establish whether theft and other counterproductive behaviors may be a problem in a job. There clearly are variations from one job to another. Only when the job analysis reveals a need for honesty testing should it be implemented.

One could quarrel in certain instances with the procedures used by Guastello and Rieke to reanalyze the data of one study or another. These reanalyses were predicated on questions regarding the approaches taken in the original studies. In some cases we would side with the investigator in the initial study, and in some cases with the reviewers. However, we are probably no more expert on these statistical concerns than the other psychologists involved. We do, however, face a problem regarding the particular studies selected for reanalysis.

Nowhere in the review is there a clear statement of the domain covered, and the extent of coverage. We have noted that this is a selective review in terms of the tests and criteria considered, but it is clearly more than that. The main focus is on studies considered in the Sackett et al. reviews of 1984 and 1989 in *Personnel Psychology*. Yet there are many apparently relevant studies that are not noted at all, and some of these studies appear to have yielded substantial validities.

We have problems with the way in which research was selected for inclusion in the review. There is much more emphasis on studies from the early 1980s, and nothing after 1989, in spite of the fact that citations to the legal literature continued to 1991. Of the studies we describe in Chapter 3 to illustrate honesty test validity, only one is considered in the review. There has been a major upgrade in research sophistication over the past 10 years. We have to conclude that, in spite of its 1991 publication date, this review is in many respects outdated. Perhaps an update would find major loopholes in the more recent research as well, but for lack of that, we believe that this review does not provide a great deal of current interest to company users of honesty tests.

The review is important, however, because it offers an understanding of the multiple approaches taken by truly dedicated adversaries of honesty tests. Reviews of this kind serve a useful purpose by stimulating thought. Whatever else they may be, such reviews are not devoid of intellectual challenge. For an application of similar modes of thinking to the polygraph, the reader should consider an article by Stephen Guastello in *The Industrial-Organizational Psychologist* (1989). A very recent statement of their position on honesty testing, although still in the same vein as the 1991 review, appears in a note by Rieke and Guastello in the *American Psychologist* (1995).

ONES, VISWESVARAN, AND SCHMIDT—1993 (POSITIVE)

Without question, this is the most comprehensive, thorough, and up-to-date review of honesty test validation. It used the techniques of meta-analysis to synthesize a wide range of findings. This review has been a long time in the making and has gone through a number of revisions. A version dated 1990 informed the American Psychological Association review. Guastello and Rieke cite a 1991 version in their paper. Kevin Murphy discusses a 1992 version in his book *Honesty in the Workplace* (1993). Daniel Seligman provides a favorable commentary in *Fortune* (1993) on the final 1993 version which was published in the *Journal of Applied Psychology*. This is the version we will consider here. It provided major input to treatments of integrity tests in the *Annual Review of Psychology* (1994) by Frank Landy, Laura Shankster, and Stacey Kohler, and in the *International Review of Industrial and Organizational Psychology* (1995) by Robert Schneider and Leaetta Hough. Both consider the review to be highly positive in its evaluation of honesty testing.

A total of 665 criterion-related validity coefficients were utilized in the meta-analysis. These derive from 180 studies and were based on an overall sample of 576,460 test takers. Extensive efforts were made to obtain information from both published sources and unpublished ones (such as test publisher technical reports). There was no meaningful difference in the level of validities from published and unpublished sources. The meta-analytic procedures followed were the standard ones, involving corrections to the data as appropriate. These corrections remove the effects of statistical and methodological artifacts and thus provide an estimate of the true validity of the tests in practice. Typically this is higher than the mean validity without corrections. In accordance with usual procedures, no corrections for social desirability or faking good were applied.

The true validity was 0.34, when the criterion was a measure of overall job performance. These studies were conducted primarily in contexts, such as retailing, where honesty considerations weigh heavily in measures of overall job performance. Not surprisingly validity is higher, at 0.47, when the criterion focuses directly on counterproductive behaviors, including theft. Both coefficients are adequate to support generalizing validity to other settings.

Looking only at the studies using an overall job performance criterion, overt integrity tests and personality-based measures are equally valid, but when the criterion becomes more directly focused on counterproductive behaviors the overt measures are superior. Concurrent studies, conducted at one point in time, appear to outperform predictive studies, where the criterion data are collected later in time. This is consistent with what has been found with other selection procedures. Nevertheless, even the predictive studies consistently yield validities in the low to mid-0.30s. When the analysis deals only with applicants, the true validity for overall job performance criteria is 0.40, and for specifically counterproductive behaviors 0.44. The tests also work just as well in jobs of high complexity, such as management, as they do in lower level positions.

There are certain additional findings that apply only when the validation strategy employs some type of counterproductive behavior as a criterion. Confessions typically yield higher validities than external measures of counterproductivity, such as established theft, presumably because the external measures capture a smaller percentage of the dishonesty actually existing. Also theft and broader indexes of counterproductivity are predicted about equally well, even by the overt integrity tests. Thus the extrapolation of honesty test results into areas such as drug and alcohol problems, production deviance and sabotage, and workplace violence appears justified. As the reviewers indicate, this may well be because what is often measured is best defined as some aspect of conscientiousness, which at its negative pole includes such things as irresponsibility, carelessness, and rule violation. Others have suggested that neuroticism may be involved as well.

DALTON, METZGER, AND WIMBUSH—1994 (NEGATIVE)

In large part, this review, published in *Research in Personnel and Human Resources Management* (1994) relies upon arguments from prior reviews. Its major conclusion is as follows:

> Two contemporaneous investigations designed to assess the validity of integrity have reached diametrically opposed conclusions. It is fair to say that one of them (Guastello and Rieke, 1991) finds such testing to be wholly without merit. Another (Ones et al., 1993) is generally supportive. At some risk of understatement, most litigators would not embrace the opportunity to be an advocate of integrity testing in the face of such alarmingly different conclusions drawn from the scientific literature. Conversely, to establish reasonable doubt about the efficacy about such testing given these disparate results would seem to be the kinder burden.
>
> While we would once again underscore the necessity for independent research establishing the base-rate for dishonest behavior, the potential adverse impact of integrity tests, and their situational moderators, we must concede that these factors do not have the priority we would accord the validity issue. Without consistent evidence of nonzero, nontrivial validities for these instruments, these other research agendas as they relate to integrity testing are largely moot. (p. 150)

Thus, although other arguments are introduced, especially one involving base rates of theft or other counterproductive behaviors and false positives, the major emphasis is on validity considerations. Furthermore, both the Guastello and Rieke and the Ones, Viswesvaran, and Schmidt reviews are repeatedly labeled as meta-analyses.

We find the following points significant:

1. The two reviews are not contemporaneous. The Guastello and Rieke analysis, although published only two years earlier, actually dealt with studies from a much earlier period when the level of research sophistication was not at its current level. Depending on the area of emphasis, the Ones, Viswesvaran, and Schmidt review is from 5 to 10 years more advanced.

2. Neither set of authors apply the term meta-analysis to the Guastello and Rieke review. The authors themselves view it as involving secondary analyses. Ones, Viswesvaran, and Schmidt specifically designate it as a literature review, and not a meta-analysis.

We would agree with these conclusions. Thus, the two reviews are not equal in this respect.

3. The scope and thoroughness of the Ones, Viswesvaran, and Schmidt review simply overwhelm that of Guastello and Rieke. By its own criteria the latter review deals with only three tests (versus 25) and focuses only on theft (versus a broad range of criteria).

4. The Dalton, Metzger, and Wimbush conclusions are couched in legalistic, rather than scientific, terms and place a strong emphasis on creating a reasonable doubt. The review strives to raise sufficient question regarding validity that employers will have second thoughts on using honesty tests because of the fear of legal reprisal. Given the data considered in this and the preceding chapters we do not consider this "reasonable doubt" argument compelling, either here or as expressed in the OTA report.

Although secondary to validity considerations, the false positive issue deserves comment because it is given considerable space in the paper. This is consistently a superstandard applied only to honesty tests. We will take up the matter in detail in later chapters. However, a quote from Dalton, Metzger, and Wimbush will place the issue in perspective:

This view (that it is inappropriate to state that, despite the validity of a selection instrument, the false positive rate may be too high) is the equivalent of stating that any selection procedure with non-zero validity is better than none at all. This view is unassailable if the sole criterion for the evaluation of a selection procedure is to reject as many unsuitable prospective employees as possible. While this may not be an unreasonable position from the perspective of an employer, critics would suggest that it fails when viewed through other lenses. (p. 143)

Given that the primary intent of this book is to provide information and education to decision makers operating "from the perspective of an employer," we believe that the false positive issue is not particularly relevant for our purposes.

CONCLUSIONS

In addition to the reviews considered in this chapter *The Mental Measurement Yearbook* in its various editions regularly contains reviews of individual honesty tests. Because these reviews discuss specific testing instruments, rather than honesty testing in general, they have not been considered here. Furthermore, the book *Honesty in the Workplace* by Kevin Murphy (1993) contains a section on the validity of honesty tests that relies heavily on the various reviews we consider. It concludes that, "although the results of recent validity studies are generally positive, these results have not quieted the controversy over integrity testing" (p. 126).

We concur with that assessment. Given the weight of the evidence, it seems to us impossible to argue that valid honesty tests cannot be, and have not been, constructed. This does not mean that any specific honesty test may not lack validity. Decision makers should seek out validity information on any test they are considering using. Since valid tests are available, it is hard to rationalize using a test when evidence for its validity is not in hand.

As Murphy notes, however, positive evidence of validities has done little to quiet the controversy. In the minds of certain people these tests are bad, and humanity should be protected from them. Strong values are involved, and the existence and use of honesty tests violates those values. Accordingly, we see little likelihood that the controversy will diminish, even in the face of more evidence for the validity of the tests. This is not to say that certain unresolved issues of a scientific nature do not remain, as Scott Lilienfeld, George Alliger, and Krystin Mitchell point out in their note in the *American Psychologist* (1995). But we believe the continuing controversy is fueled more by strong values than by unresolved scientific issues.

5

Assessing Honesty Tests: Reliability of Measurement, Question Characteristics, Test Dimensions, Applicant Reactions, and Fakability

When making a decision about using an honesty test, the most important thing to look for is demonstrated validity for people and purposes as similar as possible to those you will use the test with and for. The evidence from meta-analyses is useful, but it will not replace knowing that a test really will accomplish what you want in organizations like yours.

After validity, however, there are a number of other aspects of the tests that are important. Test publishers tend to discuss them, especially if they have evidence on the matter, and they should. If they do not, then inquiries should be made. Either way, these are considerations, inherent in the tests themselves, about which a decision maker needs information before deciding to adopt a test. The five factors noted in the title of this chapter do involve some requirements for psychological measurement and statistical understanding, but none of these requirements are any more complex than those involved in understanding the validation process set forth in Chapter 3.

Although there is no real substitute for having detailed information on these topics, something one should learn about in any event is the professional stature of the psychologist(s) involved. Who created the test items and did the test development work? The more signs of professional stature on the resumé, the more likely it is that an individual has been evaluated favorably by his or her peers. A Ph.D. from a major university, holding important professional positions either in the academic world or business, state licensure as a psychologist, and publications are important. Where the publications appear is important also. An idea of what to look for may be gained from the citations sprinkled throughout this book, and presented in full in the Bibliography.

Membership, holding office, and fellow status in relevant professional associations is another consideration. These associations would include the American

Psychological Association, the Society for Industrial and Organizational Psychology, the American Psychological Society, the Academy of Management, and the Society for Personality Assessment. Other evidence of professional accomplishment should be taken into account as well. A detailed discussion on this subject is contained in an article by Robin Inwald in *Personnel Journal* (1988). The important point is that it is appropriate to ask for resumés, and to spend time evaluating them. In our experience, this is done much less frequently than it should be.

Keep in mind, however, that younger professionals may well have fewer credentials, simply because they are new to the field. In such cases it is appropriate to ask about the accomplishments of supervisors or mentors who might be assisting with the person's work.

RELIABILITY OF MEASUREMENT

Reliability means that if one makes the same measurement twice, the same result will be obtained both times. To the extent that this is not true, the measure is said to be unreliable. Thus, if one uses a ruler made of wood or metal to measure a distance twice, it is probable that almost identical results will be obtained. But if one tries to do the same thing with a thin rubber ruler, the results will depend on the tension induced, and the two measures may not yield the same result at all. Unfortunately, psychological measurement often seems to be like the situation with the rubber ruler: Consistency or stability of measurement may be quite low, making it very difficult to achieve successful prediction. Unreliability in an honesty test can serve to constrain validity so that a significant coefficient is not obtained.

A variety of procedures have been developed to measure reliability, although the typical outcome, a correlation coefficient, is the same in all cases. The various procedures tend to yield somewhat different values for this reliability coefficient, but the results should be sufficiently close so that the procedures may be considered interchangeable for practical purposes. It is important to understand, however, that reliability and validity are not the same thing, even though both are typically expressed as correlation coefficients. In the honesty-test marketplace this distinction is not always maintained, and since reliability coefficients tend to be much higher than validity coefficients, considerable misunderstanding can result.

In the test-retest procedure for determining reliability, a second measurement is required at some time subsequent to the first; then the scores obtained in the two time periods are correlated. Thus, the same test data must be collected at two different points in time, and a major question relates to the interval between these measurements. It is essential that this interval be sufficient so that memory effects are unlikely to influence the results. However, too long an interval increasingly confounds true change in people, with unreliability of measurement. The answer to the interval question, then, is that the measures should be taken as close together as possible without memory compromising independence.

One way of avoiding this independence problem is to use two different measures of the same construct. Because the questions are actually different, memory effects cannot operate, and the two forms may be used with a very short time interval between them. The problem, however, with this parallel form procedure is that two tests must be developed rather than one, and they both must be shown to yield the same results.

Precise statistical definitions establishing the requirements for a parallel form have been advanced. However, for working purposes, parallel forms are said to exist where (1) the number of items of each type is the same, so that the measures concentrate equally on the same aspects of the individual; (2) the average scores tend to be essentially the same; and (3) the distributions of actual scores through the range of possible scores are roughly comparable. Whether these conditions can be met, and in fact whether a parallel measure can be developed at all, depends largely on the nature of the measure involved. In honesty testing it is rare to find two tests that meet all of these conditions, and thus qualify as true parallel forms, even though a number of tests exist in multiple editions or versions. Thus, parallel form reliability is not something one is likely to encounter in this field.

A widely used approximation to the parallel form procedure involves splitting an existing measure into two equal parts and then correlating the scores on these parts to obtain an estimate of reliability. For example, one can use the odd-numbered items as one measure and the even-numbered ones as another. Procedures of this type which actually utilize only one test and single administrations of that test are referred to as internal consistency reliability approaches.

Where internal consistency is established using split halves (such as the odd-even procedure), an additional step is required beyond simply correlating the scores for the two halves. A measure tends to become more reliable as more measurements are added. In the case of honesty tests this means questions. When the split-half method is used to calculate reliability, the number of measurements is actually cut in half. Thus a correction must be applied to bring the reliability coefficient up to where it would be with a test twice as long as the two halves. There is a simple formula for this purpose.

There are many ways to split a test into two equal parts. The average of all possible such splits is called coefficient alpha, and it is currently the most widely used measure of reliability.

The most extensive investigation of the reliability of honesty tests is contained in the review by Ones, Viswesvaran, and Schmidt (1993). There the mean coefficient alpha was 0.81, and the test-retest mean was 0.85. Michael O'Bannon, Linda Goldinger, and Gavin Appleby (1989) argue that the test-retest procedure is more appropriate to the practical demands of honesty test usage, a position with which we would agree; they report figures based on this procedure only. The average coefficient from the studies they considered was 0.88.

From these data one would expect to find in the typical case, evidence of test-retest reliability in the mid to high 0.80s; ideally this figure would be in the 0.90s. Below these values extending down to about 0.70, group comparisons can be made without difficulty. However, honesty testing for selection involves decisions about individuals, and there reliabilities in the 0.90s are desired.

Actually, the range of these coefficients across tests varies considerably. Personality-based measures appear to produce somewhat lower reliabilities than the overt tests, perhaps because the items appear more ambiguous to those taking the tests. Thus a person may respond one way the first time and another way the second. Also, tests that have multiple scales for theft, violence, drug abuse, accident proneness, emotional instability, and the like often have relatively few questions in any one scale, and the reliability coefficients for these separate scales tend to be lower as a result.

A number of the points we have been making can be illustrated using data from our own experiences. Our test was of the overt nature and was relatively long, containing 82 items. The test was administered twice to 62 typical applicants for jobs in a number of different companies. The mean interval was 30 days. However, 61 percent were retested within a week and another 16 percent before the first month was over. The longest interval between testings was almost eight months. There was no evidence that the scores were more alike with the shorter intervals.

The reliability coefficient obtained under these circumstances was was 0.98, a very high figure but still not unheard of elsewhere in the honesty testing field. The relationship between scores at first and second testing is depicted in Table 5.1. The means and standard deviations at the two points in time were essentially the same. This is an important point, because on some kinds of tests practice with the questions causes the scores to increase on the second testing. This can happen even when the reliability coefficient is quite high, but more frequently the practice effects differ from person to person, and the coefficient obtained underestimates the true reliability somewhat.

At one point, under pressure from the competition, we developed a shorter version of our test, half as long, which contained those questions that discriminated best between honest and dishonest people as determined by the polygraph. This 41-question test had a test-retest reliability of 0.96, exactly what one would predict using the formula to estimate the impact of reduced test length. Validity against a polygraph criterion dropped from 0.69 to 0.61.

In this instance both reliability and validity remained high with the shorter test. However, this result cannot always be assumed. Clients tend to prefer short tests, especially if they are screening large numbers of applicants and using a variety of selection procedures. But there are risks to pushing this strategy too far. If the reliability of the longer test is already down in the 0.80s, reduced test length can be expected to have more impact, much more than the change of

Table 5.1
Relationship between Honesty Test Scores at First and Second Testing (Reliability = 0.98)

Scores—First Testing	Second Testing										
	36-38	39-41	42-44	45-47	48-50	51-53	54-56	57-59	60-62	63-65	66-68
66-68										1	
63-65										1	2
60-62									5		
57-59								2			
54-56						1	1	1			
51-53					1	3	1				
48-50				4	1	1					
45-47			1	2	2						
42-44		4	8	9							
39-41	1	6									
36-38	2	2									

0.02 points we found with a very high reliability. As a result validity will suffer as well. It is often assumed that reliability remains the same as a test is shortened, and thus there is a failure to establish values for the new, shorter test. Yet this is incorrect. If at all possible, it is better to use a longer test. If a shorter version looks attractive, it is essential to establish the reliability and validity of that specific test. These and other considerations related to reliability are discussed in the first author's book entitled *Industrial-Organizational Psychology* (1992).

QUESTION CHARACTERISTICS AND TEST DEVELOPMENT

The first honesty test was developed for use by the Army during World War II to screen inductees for military service. The author, Gilbert Betts, was at the time a military officer. Subsequently, the test was revised and made available to employers. However, in the late 1950s, at a time when the outcry against personality testing was particularly intense, it was withdrawn from the market because of a fear of lawsuits. Although well developed and based on extensive research, with validities in the 0.50s, it has never been reintroduced in the marketplace.

The test was of the overt integrity type and contained items such as the following:

How often do you tell lies?

Ever expelled from school?

Ever in trouble with the law, sent to correctional school?

Do you feel that you have more trouble keeping a job than most people?

How much can most people be trusted?

Do you feel that you are very "trustworthy" (honest and responsible)?

The history of this instrument is described in an article by Philip Ash and Samuel Maurice in the *Journal of Business and Psychology* (1988) and again by Ash in chapter 1 of John Jones's edited volume *Preemployment Honesty Testing* (1991a).

Dan Dalton, Michael Metzger, and James Wimbush, writing in *Research in Personnel and Human Resources Management* (1994), provide additional illustrations of honesty test questions drawn from various sources, including the Office of Technology Assessment report and an article by G. A. Hanson in *Law and Inequality* (1991). These illustrations are categorized using the O'Bannon, Goldinger, and Appleby classifications noted in the Introduction; examples of overt and veiled-purpose questions are provided as well.

Questions involving admissions of illegal or disapproved activities (confessions) might take the following form:

Which drugs have you tried and how often?

If you could write a check for everything you have taken from a former employer without paying for it, it would be for $ _____ .

I have done something that has made me feel disgusted with myself.

I have never been convicted of a crime.

I have never lied to someone who trusted me.

Opinions toward illegal or disapproved behavior (honesty attitudes) can be obtained as follows:

Most people will take a day off from work and lie about it by saying they are sick.

An employer should look to why an employee steals rather than to call him or her a liar.

These days, smoking a marijuana cigarette is about the same as drinking a cup of coffee.

I believe that most people are two-faced.

Do you think company bosses get away with more things than their employees?

Descriptions of one's own personality and thought patterns (self reports) can be as follows:

My hardest battles are with myself.

I wish I could be as happy as others seem to be.

I am sure I am being talked about.

How often do you blush?

I am not afraid of fire.

Reactions to hypothetical situations (scenarios) can be of the following types:

Your boss docks you 10 dollars because as a checker you took a 10 dollar bad check. It is morally all right to take 10 dollars from the company because they took 10 dollars from you.

Tom is a very good employee. One day, however, he smokes marijuana during his lunch break and returns to work too high to do his job. He should be: (a) fired, (b) suspended without pay, (c) given a warning.

Overt, or clear-purpose, tests usually use questions of the first (confession), second (honesty attitude), or fourth (scenario) type. Other examples of such questions are:

How many people have cheated the government on their income tax returns?

Do you believe most employers take advantage of the people who work for them?

How much do you dislike doing what someone tells you to do?

How easy is it to get away with stealing?

Do you think it is stealing to take small items home from work?

Veiled-purpose questions of the kind used in personality-based tests are likely to be of the third (self-report) type, such as the following:

How many people don't like you?

I feel lonely when I am with other people.

I like to create excitement.

I like to take chances.

A lot of times I went against my parents' wishes.

In the test with which we were involved, there were a number of scenario items which use the following format:

Jane works as a sales clerk in a store beside the Interstate Highway. The store's customers are mostly tourists who stop to buy gasoline, snacks, and souvenirs. One day Jane accidentally gives a man change for a $10 bill when he actually had given her a $20 bill. After the man left, Jane saw the $20 bill in the cash drawer with the tens and realized what she had done. At this point Jane might react in several ways. Indicate whether you agree with each of these possibilities.

1. Jane decides to deny that she shortchanged the customer if he returns for his $10. That will save her a lot of embarrassment. Do you agree?
   Yes _____   No _____

2. Jane regrets the incident, but decides to make the best of a bad situation. She takes $10 from the cash drawer and tells her supervisor she is sick and wants the rest of the day off. Do you agree?
   Yes _____   No _____

3. Jane will gladly return the $10 to the customer if she sees him again. Meanwhile, she turns the extra money over to the store manager and decides to make up for the mistake by contributing $10 of her own money to a local charity. Do you agree?
   Yes _____   No _____

4. Jane turns the extra money over to the store at the end of her shift because the customer has not returned. She also writes down everything she can remember about how the man looks. If he ever stops at the store again, she will repay him with her own money. Do you agree?
   Yes _____   No _____

Confession and honesty attitude questions such as the following make up the remainder of the test:

If I saw a person accidentally throw away a winning ticket at a race track, I would hand it back to that person.

Yes _____   No _____

If I got caught stealing, I think I should be given another chance if it was the first time it ever happened.

Yes _____   No _____

Have you cheated on the number of hours you have worked for any employer?

Yes _____   No _____

Our test may also be used to illustrate one way in which questions are selected for a test. We started with a large number of items of the scenario type administered to a substantial number of job applicants who completed the polygraph as well. However, as it turned out the scenario procedure operates somewhat differently from other types of overt items; we did not know that in the beginning. Thus, what we got was a large number of response patterns that looked essentially as follows:

	Responses among those who *passed* the polygraph, in answering the honesty test		Responses among those who *failed* the polygraph, in answering the honesty test	
Response	Yes	No	Yes	No
Percent	50	50	48	52

In short, among the applicants overall, there was very little difference in the honesty test responses of those who were believed to be honest and those who were not. The polygraph results, scored by an experienced polygraph examiner and instructor (Michael Capps), were categorized using the following scale:

1. No marijuana use in the past year; no hard drug use ever; no drug sales, no convictions; no serious undetected crime; no theft of money from any previous employer, no theft of more than $20 in merchandise per year from any previous employer, no single item of more than $5; no current alcohol problem.

2. Has used marijuana in the last year, but not on a weekly basis; has not used hard drugs within the last year; has not sold drugs ever; no convictions, no serious undetected crimes; no money theft from previous employer; no theft of merchandise of more than $100 per year, or no single item of $10 or more from any previous employer; no current alcohol problem.

3. Uses marijuana no more than twice a week; has smoked marijuana on the job but not in the last year. Has used hard drugs, but not in the last year; used cocaine less than once a month; has stolen money from a previous employer, but less than $20 in a year; has stolen merchandise from a previous employer, but less than $200 in a year.

4. Uses marijuana four or five days a week; used marijuana on the last job, or on the current job; has used hard drugs within the past year; uses cocaine on a monthly basis; has stolen more than $20 in money in a year from some previous employer; has stolen

more than $200 in merchandise in a year from some previous employer; has been convicted of a felony or of other crimes involving theft, or has attitudinal problems which would have a bearing on the job; participation in crimes of a like nature in which the person was not caught.

In general, category 1 responses were used to establish *passing* the polygraph exam and category 4 responses to indicate *failing*. Thus, there was a large difference on the polygraph between the two groups. In spite of the minimal differences overall on the scenario questions, however, we found much larger differences when we looked at new samples from the various race and sex groups, and made similar comparisons. Among black women, for instances, we might find the following:

	Responses among those who *passed* the polygraph, in answering the honesty test		Responses among those who *failed* the polygraph, in answering the honesty test	
Response	Yes	No	Yes	No
Percent	90	10	72	28

This type of finding was repeated often enough that it was possible to construct a meaningful scale for each of the four race and sex groups. These scales were far from being the same; response discrimination frequently occurred on different questions, or if the question was the same, to different degrees, and even sometimes in different directions. Yet we had the makings of a test, even though when we carried out an independent validation using the items that distinguished honest from dishonest people, the overall correlation with a polygraph criterion was only 0.34.

At this point we took another, new group of questions—some of the scenario type and many more of the confession and honesty attitude type—and did the whole study over again with new samples. Now the polygraph correlation was 0.51. Clearly the confession and honesty attitude questions were adding something above and beyond the validity of the scenario questions. Furthermore, these questions, unlike the scenarios, showed relatively little difference in the way they operated from one race-sex group to another.

Finally, we selected those questions from the two studies that distinguished the best between honest and dishonest people (as indicated by the polygraph) and carried out an independent validation in a new sample. The result was a validity of 0.69. During this lengthy process we discarded a number of questions that never did distinguish very well between honest and dishonest people in any race-sex group. We also established a weighted scoring system for those questions retained in the final test, based on how well the question discriminated between honest and dishonest people.

This weighting process gave a higher score on a question to those responses that were better at distinguishing honest from dishonest individuals. Thus two questions might produce response patterns as follows:

Question 1.	**Passed polygraph**		**Failed polygraph**	
Response	Yes	No	Yes	No
Percent	65	35	52	48

Question 2.	**Passed polygraph**		**Failed polygraph**	
Response	Yes	No	Yes	No
Percent	65	35	40	60

Question 2 would yield a higher score, contributing more to the total, because it discriminated to a greater extent between honest and dishonest people.

These weights were established using the percentage differences—such as 13 for Question 1 and 25 for Question 2. It is also common practice to calculate the correlation between the scores on each question and an external criterion—in this case the polygraph result. Any item that yields a very low correlation is discarded, and among those retained for the final test, the higher the correlation the larger the weighted score attached to a particular response.

The example described uses another external test—the polygraph—to select and weight items. It is also possible to use another honesty test that has been previously validated in exactly the same manner. Thus, if one has an already established overt integrity test and wishes to develop a personality-based measure, perhaps for use with top executives, a large number of self-report questions may be administered along with the overt test, and the former analyzed in relation to the overt test results, just as we did using the polygraph.

Similarly, the external criterion used to develop the test may be supervisory ratings, background investigations, detected theft, and the like; it need not be another test. Gilbert Betts, in developing the first honesty test, compared various questions with an external criterion which utilized three groups of soldiers consisting of nonoffenders, offenders, and recidivists (multiple offenders). Thus, the military court system served to establish the criterion groupings. Questions that distinguished one group from another most effectively were retained in the final test.

All of these approaches use some type of external criterion to assess honesty in some form. Then items that best predict this criterion are selected. On occasion, however, item selection is carried out using the total score obtained from all questions initially under consideration. Because there are many questions, this internal criterion is likely to be reliable, and the effects of any poor items are diluted in the composite. Each item score is correlated with the composite score, and those questions that correlate most highly are retained. The result is inevitably a test with high internal consistency reliability. Yet, if there are initial problems in conceptualizing the measure and writing questions to tap the concept, validity may be lacking. It is entirely possible to develop a very good test of something that has no practical relevance at all. Only subsequent validation will tell.

In evaluating an honesty test, it is crucial to know how the test was developed. How were questions selected and keyed? What type of criterion was used in the item analysis? It is entirely possible that no external or internal criterion was used, and that items were selected and even weighted based on somebody's rational expectations. That can mean problems. If an internal criterion is used, external validity may be low, or absent. When an external criterion is applied to select and weight items, the nature of that criterion defines the nature of the test. Thus scrutiny of the criterion becomes a key element in establishing who the test will screen out and select in.

TEST DIMENSIONS AND FACTOR STRUCTURE

Studies have been conducted with a number of honesty tests to determine what the tests measure, using an analysis of the questions themselves for this purpose. Generally this requires what is called a ''factor analysis'' on the items. The fact that such an analysis has been carried out may be used to promote the test. Thus, it is important to understand this procedure.

Factor analysis is a method of studying the general characteristics measured by a test's questions. There are a number of mathematical procedures that may be followed, but all examine the pattern of relationships or correlations among test questions. Thus the starting point is a correlation matrix in which each item is correlated with every other. Then techniques are applied to identify clusters of items which are highly related to one another, and thus combine to measure dimensions of personality or behavior. When the clusters that are most pronounced within the questions of a test have been identified, the specific questions within each cluster are examined to establish meanings. What do these items have in common that would account for their emergence as a test dimension? In this way factors are labeled.

It is possible that the questions in a test might all be closely interrelated and thus only a single factor is identified. However, that is not typical with honesty tests. Various studies have identified from three to seven factors or dimensions, depending on the specific questions included in the test. Furthermore, even when different tests yield the same number of factors, they need not be the same ones.

By way of illustration let us consider two different tests. The first study was conducted by Michael Harris and Paul Sackett and published in the *Journal of Business and Psychology* (1989). The test contained 40 questions, and the factor analysis was carried out using the responses of 849 applicants for positions as retail sales clerks. Four factors were obtained, although the first was by far the most pervasive. This dimension dealt with a person's temptations and thoughts about dishonest activities, such as being tempted to steal merchandise or money. The second dimension contained items reflecting actual or expected dishonest activities by an individual, such as illegally taking company property. The third dimension reflected the person's norms about what others do when it comes to dishonest activities, such as their expectations regarding how many people engage in criminal activity. The fourth dimension contained self-report questions related to the person's impulsiveness and reliability.

The second study was published in the same journal and was carried out by Michael Cunningham and Philip Ash. Although there were four interpretable factors (a fifth proved to be uninterpretable), no single factor appeared to contain a majority of the items, as in the previous instance. The study under consideration involved a 70-item test given to 1,281 job applicants for a diverse array of positions. The first dimension reflected a general tendency to oppose or avoid punishing and disciplining other people. The second dimension reflected self-indulgence and an unwillingness to punish either oneself or friends and family members in the event of misbehavior. The third dimension reflected fantasies of dishonest behavior or speculation about performing dishonestly. The fourth dimension reflected views as to the likelihood that others might behave dishonestly.

There are certain similarities, but major differences as well between the dimensions identified in the two tests. The fact that both are overt integrity tests does not mean that factor analysis will yield identical results. Evidence from factor analyses of other tests suggests that there is no one honesty factor. The tests overlap in the factors they measure. Most tests seem to tap at least some dimensions that are different from those in other tests. Accordingly, there could be some gain from using more than one honesty test, especially if separate scores are created for the various dimensions. Furthermore, there may be reason to shop around for a test that contains dimensions that best fit the needs of a particular company. If the results of factor analyses are available for a test, that facilitates this process.

The idea that conscientiousness may be the overriding dimension in honesty tests is a view that we have noted at several points, and it is obviously relevant to the present discussion. The best evidence on the matter comes from a study by Kevin Murphy and Sandra Lee reported in the *Journal of Business and Psychology* (1994). Two honesty tests, one overt and one personality-based, were administered to 180 university students along with two measures of conscientiousness and a general personality inventory that deals with multiple characteristics. The conscientiousness measures correlated significantly with all of the honesty test scores, with an average correlation of 0.34. This was the highest such figure obtained with any of the personality characteristics measured (the next highest was 0.26). Yet other characteristics did show a number of significant relationships with honesty test scores.

The authors reached four conclusions:

1. The correlations between integrity and conscientiousness measures are for the most part modest, suggesting that these measures cannot be used interchangeably.

2. Conscientiousness is not the only facet of normal personality that might be useful in understanding integrity test scores.

3. Personality constructs are likely to be more useful in understanding some types of integrity tests than others (particularly personality-based).

4. No single personality trait will be sufficient for explaining integrity, but the trait conscientiousness is likely to be an important component of any adequate theory of integrity.

Since honesty tests were developed originally from relationships with the polygraph, confessions, and convictions, rather than from any particular theory of integrity, this is not a surprising set of conclusions.

APPLICANT REACTIONS AND IMPRESSIONS

Increasingly, concerns have been raised regarding the questions asked in honesty tests and whether they "turn people off" so that they feel negatively disposed to the companies that ask such questions, or even refuse to take the tests at all. A major text on selection (*Staffing Organizations* by Herbert and Robert Heneman, 1994) for example, has raised just this issue.

Sara Rynes and Mary Connerley, writing in the *Journal of Business and Psychology* (1993) compared the reactions to honesty tests of almost 400 university students with their reactions to 12 other selection devices. In general, the responses to honesty tests were about neutral, ranging very close to the midpoint on the scale on several different evaluative questions. Furthermore, honesty tests ranked in the mid-range among the various selection procedures considered, which included interviews, other tests, references, handwriting analyses, simulations, and drug tests. The students did not feel strongly either in a positive or negative sense regarding companies that used honesty tests.

Yet Sara Rynes does not say this in her chapter in *Personnel Selection in Organizations* (1993) edited by Neal Schmitt and Walter Borman. She notes a variety of student criticisms of honesty test items and says "even the most cursory examination of some of the most commonly used instruments reveals a striking number of highly personal, seemingly irrelevant, and potentially sexist or racially divisive items" (p. 250). If this were true, one would think the students in her survey would have revealed more negative reactions to honesty tests.

Another study by Ann Ryan and Paul Sackett and published in the *Journal of Business and Psychology* (1987) asked students for their reactions to honesty tests in the abstract, not relative to other selection procedures. The questioning was quite extensive, and produced the following results:

68% felt it was appropriate for an employer to administer such a test.

10% would refuse to take such a test.

25% would enjoy being asked to take such a test.

42% felt this type of test was an invasion of privacy.

46% said if they had two comparable job offers, they would reject the company using such a test.

26% would resent being asked to take such a test.

59% felt that a test such as this is sometimes an appropriate selection procedure.

33% believe that administering a test such as this reflects negatively on the organization.

42% indicated that being asked to take such a test would not affect their view of the organization.

56% indicated that tests such as this are routinely used in industry.

Again the reaction is mixed. However, the respondents are college students, not job applicants. Furthermore, these students are unlikely to be candidates for the jobs for which honesty tests are most frequently used. When it comes to the hard realities of actually obtaining a position, some of this negativism may evaporate.

It is important to note the results of another comparison in which the college students who took an honesty test as part of a simulated selection process were compared with students who completed a selection process from which the honesty test was deleted. The students were then asked to rate their views of the organization involved. On 21 of the 23 rating characteristics there was no difference. However, organizations using honesty tests were perceived to provide less feedback and to utilize closer supervision—thus to be somewhat more controlling. Overall, the honesty test did not appear to make a great deal of difference.

In chapter 9 of the book by John Jones entitled *Preemployment Honesty Testing* (1991a), the author describes two studies conducted with job applicants. In the first, the applicants were asked to note any comments they might have after completing an overt honesty test. Objections of some kind were noted by 18 percent. However, some of these objections applied to any test, not just the honesty type. Thus, the 18 percent may be something of an overstatement of objections to honesty testing per se. The study also found that objections were most prevalent among those whom the test found to be dishonest. This was true even though the tests had not even been scored at the time the objections occurred.

The second study was conducted using manager trainee applicants to a fast food restaurant chain. This study employed a version of the questionnaire Ryan and Sackett used to assess reactions to the testing. Comparisons of the two sets of results, although not based on identical honesty tests, are feasible given that both tests were overt in nature. The results among the management job applicants were as follows:

Table 5.2
Answer to the Question: Did You Find This Questionnaire to Be Offensive?

State	Number of Applicants	Percent Indicating *Yes*	Mean Test Score for *Yes* Respondents
California	103	4	51.8
Florida	475	5	51.8
Georgia	327	4	52.9
New York	170	7	48.9
Total	1,075	5	51.4

90% felt it was appropriate for an employer to administer such a test.

4% would refuse to take such a test.

63% would enjoy being asked to take such a test.

11% felt this type of test was an invasion of privacy.

2% said if they had two comparable job offers, they would reject the company using such a test.

3% would resent being asked to take such a test.

82% felt that a test such as this is sometimes an appropriate selection procedure.

5% believe that administering a test such as this reflects negatively on the organization.

80% indicated that being asked to take such a test would not affect their view of the organization.

80% indicated that tests such as this are routinely used in industry.

On all 10 questions, the job applicants were more favorably disposed to the honesty test than the students, the average difference amounting to over 25% per question. In general, the applicants did not express major objections to the test. Again, as in the first study, poor test performance and negative reactions to the honesty test were related.

Working with our own test, we have information of a similar nature from four states as indicated in Table 5.2. A Yes answer to the question, "Did you find this questionnaire to be offensive?" occurred very close to 5 percent of the time, irrespective of the region of the country involved. Again the test was an overt one; all respondents were job applicants. As indicated in the last column of Table 5.2, we did not find particularly low scores among those who indicated objections. Since the mean score on the test is 50, those who felt the test was offensive actually scored slightly, but not significantly, above average. Why we do not obtain the same result as Jones reported is not clear to us. It may have to do with the way in which objections were indicated; it could have some relationship to the approach used in developing the two honesty tests, and thus establishing their scores.

It is apparent that in appropriate applicant groups, objections to honesty tests are not nearly as great as some writers on the subject seem to anticipate. A study by John Jones in the *Journal of Business and Psychology* (1991b) suggests one reason. Questions contained in overt and personality-based tests were compared as to their judged job-relatedness, offensiveness, and invasiveness. The personality-based items were often viewed as more offensive and invasive; they were also considered to be less job-related.

It appears that job applicants expect to be asked questions related to the work to be performed. If that work involves opportunities for theft and other counterproductive behavior, then asking questions about such matters is not felt to be inappropriate. Thus, the overt tests fail to stir the negative reactions in applicants that they sometimes do in others, who are not considering the tests in relation to a specific position. Most personality-based tests do not have this quality of job-relatedness. For some purposes that may be advantageous, but not always. Even the items from the two personality-based tests that John Jones studied were judged to be essentially neutral, not highly offensive.

One of the personality-based tests Jones studied was, in fact, used in some mail-survey research conducted by Steven Kobbs and Richard Arvey and published in the *Journal of Business and Psychology* (1993). Comparisons were made between the test scores of nurses who had official actions taken against their nursing licenses by the Minnesota Board of Nursing (often for drug use) and a group among whom no such actions had been taken. One would expect the deviant nurses to score lower on the test, and they did; the validity coefficient was 0.34. However, what is of interest for present purposes was the response rate. Among the deviant nurses 63 percent of those contacted completed the test. Among those who did not have a blemish on their license the rate was 51 percent. These are very good response rates for a mail survey of this kind. They do not appear to indicate that the nurses were offended in large numbers by the test questions. If they had been, far fewer would have completed the tests.

From years of experience we know that many people do not like psychological tests. Yet they have come to live with them, and to view them as appropriate, even useful, for many selection purposes. So it is with honesty tests. Everything that has been learned to date indicates that there is no great outcry against these tests among the people who are most affected by them. From an employer viewpoint it is also important that using the tests, especially those of the overt variety, in situations where they are appropriate can convey a message that the company cares about the things the test measures. Thus a climate for honesty may be fostered.

FAKABILITY AND RESPONDING WITH A SOCIALLY DESIRABLE ANSWER

In the preceding chapter we touched upon the problem of faking by giving socially desirable answers rather than true ones. This matter of faking good was a particular concern in the review by Stephen Guastello and Mark Rieke. Now we want to return to this issue and give it more attention.

A number of honesty test publishers have developed special scales for their tests designed to detect individuals who in one way or another may distort their answers to "beat the test." The most common approach to beating the tests is to fake good and thus present oneself in a favorable light by selecting the most socially desirable answers. When an applicant provides evidence of such faking on a special scale the best approach is to discount the test completely, rather than attempt to apply some type of correction to the score obtained. The individual is told that the test did not yield a good reading and that a second administration will be required. This is the preferred approach, and in most cases the signs of faking disappear on the second testing.

Special scales of this kind are developed in several ways. One procedure is to ask a group of test-takers to respond so as to make themselves look as attractive as possible, to fake good. The answers of these people are then compared with those of some other group, such as people asked to respond as truthfully as possible. Those items which clearly differentiate the two groups are then selected for inclusion in the special scale. The scale thus developed is a "fake-good" scale.

As several investigators have found, including Ann Ryan and Paul Sackett writing in the *Journal of Business and Psychology* (1987), people can distort their answers and present themselves favorably on overt integrity tests. The Ryan and Sackett study used an experimental test that is not commercially available. However, Carol Dean, Charles Ramser, and Al Krienke report a similar result in the *Southern Management Association Proceedings* (1995), and in this case two standard commercial tests were used. Both of these studies were carried out with students, not job applicants. Steven LoBello and Benjamin Sims, in the *Journal of Business and Psychology* (1993), report that prisoners can fake good, and that a number produce test scores at a level sufficient to warrant employment. There is also evidence from the research of Michael Cunningham, Dennis Wong, and Anita Barbee reported in the *Journal of Applied Psychology* (1994) that job applicants seeking employment may well respond with socially desirable answers, at least to some degree, and thus may in fact fake good to an extent.

This same research, however, makes it clear that in spite of this, validity is not affected. The scores are shifted upward, but even so the order of scores remains roughly the same and the validity coefficient is not affected to any marked degree. This is consistent with our conclusion in Chapter 4. Where tests have been developed by selecting items and weighting them using some external criterion, such as the polygraph or evidence of theft, much of the social desirability effect is removed. Items subject to distortion on this ground are either eliminated or receive low weights. To the extent a test is keyed to external criteria, validity will be reduced very little by social desirability bias. In many cases, as with the test we collaborated on, it may not be reduced at all.

Procedures for incorporating special scales in tests to detect social desirability

Table 5.3
Frequency Counts for Different Score Levels on a Scale Consisting of Answers Most Often Given (34 Items in All)

	Frequency Count Among 70,986 Job Applicants	
Scale Score	**Number**	**Percent**
0-9	32	.05
10-19	638	.90
20-24	1,895	2.67
25-29	9,591	13.51
30	5,389	7.59
31	8,124	11.44
32	11,770	16.58
33	16,921	23.84
All 34	16,626	23.42

distortion have been around for some time. Robert Guion described approaches of this kind in his book *Personnel Testing* in 1965. When such scales are used, and also because social desirability tends to have little impact on validity in any event, faking good appears to be a minimal problem.

Although developing special scales from the responses of people instructed to fake good is a common procedure, there are other ways of dealing with the same problem. One procedure is to construct a scale made up of the most frequently selected answers, on the assumption that those who fake good will be attracted to these more socially desirable responses. Thus a scale can be developed which includes all answers given by more than, say, 50 percent of those taking the test. Table 5.3 shows how this type of scale will yield very few low scores and a great many at the high end—simply because the scale contains answers that are given very frequently. In this instance, based on our data, almost 50 percent of the test-takers have scores of 33 or 34.

Special scales to detect faking are not limited to those that focus on social desirability. As Alan Frost and Joseph Orban note in their *Journal of Business and Psychology* article (1990), respondents can answer in various ways designed to beat the test, or at least to be unresponsive to it. Usually these patterns result in very low scores, suggesting a lack of honesty, but they do not necessarily reflect true dishonesty. Thus, a person who goes through a test simply answering at random, or pretending not to understand the items, would likely endorse a number of very infrequently selected answers, and obtain a score indicative of dishonesty without having actually read or deliberated upon the items at all. When this type of distortion occurs often, validity can be compromised.

Detecting distortion of this type can be achieved with a scale such as that utilized to construct Table 5.3. Low scores on such a measure, in this case scores of 19 or lower, can provide evidence for random responding having no relationship to the real content of the questions. Alternatively, scales may be constructed of very rarely selected answers, in which case high scores would indicate the distortion. In our data this approach to beating the test appears less than 1 percent of the time. However, should the approach be used frequently, it would completely defeat the purpose of testing. Thus, having a special scale to detect this type of distortion is worthwhile.

We conclude that incorporating special scales in a test to identify faking and distortion of one kind or another is highly desirable. If such scales are not in existence, then research evidence should be provided that they are not needed. This is a factor that should be taken into account in evaluating a test. For those who wish more detailed information on matters of response distortion and faking in personality testing generally, we would suggest a reading of the *Journal of Applied Psychology* monograph (1990) by Leaetta Hough, Newell Eaton, Marvin Dunnette, John Kamp, and Rodney McCloy. The evidence presented there provides considerable support for our interpretations.

CONCLUSIONS

In this chapter we have considered a number of aspects of honesty tests, extending beyond validity. Information should be obtained on test reliability, including how reliability was measured. The way in which the test was originally developed needs to be ascertained, as well as whether and how new questions were subsequently added and weights changed. Although data on the factor structure of a test and indications of what the test measures (obtained by correlating it with other tests) are not essential, they can be useful. It may be that the best approach for a particular company would be to use several honesty tests, each of which measures a somewhat different set of dimensions.

Applicant reactions to honesty test items are usually not a problem, especially if the test is obviously job-related. However, it is a good idea to take a close look at the items contained in any given test, and to obtain information on how applicants have reacted in the past if there is any concern. Many tests contain special scales to identify respondents who have answered primarily in terms of social desirability, rather than honesty, or who have resorted to faking in some other form. Information on the existence and need for such scales should be obtained.

These issues are often featured in the promotional material of test publishers, if they have been addressed. However, the most reliable source on concerns of this type is the professional literature. Journal articles and books typically are reviewed, usually anonymously, by other professionals before being published. The system may not be fully objective in all cases, but it can be expected to be more objective than the promotional material of test publishers. Thus, a search of the literature to find information of the kind we have been considering on a particular test is strongly recommended.

Second, we recommend that the professional qualifications and stature of those who developed the test and worked on it be considered. This requires a close reading of resumés. There is a skill inherent in this process, but it is not much different when the resumé describes a psychologist than when a job applicant of some other kind is involved. The important point is to obtain the resumé and study it.

6

Using Honesty Tests: Establishing
Cutting Scores, Dealing with the False
Positive Problem, Training Users,
and Identifying Barriers to Testing

In Chapter 5 we considered aspects of the tests that need to be taken into account in making decisions about the test to use. Now we take up a series of issues related to the way in which tests are used. These are matters in which test publishers may or may not involve themselves. Yet ultimately they are matters that users should take into their own hands, and thus for which they should assume responsibility. If users do not, it is unlikely that they will get as much out of their investment in the testing as they could.

ESTABLISHING CUTTING SCORES

A cutting score on an honesty test is the score below which applicants will not be hired, assuming that high scores reflect a greater amount of honesty. If cutting scores are set very low there will be little selection; almost everyone who applies will be considered eligible for hiring. If the cut is made at a very high level most applicants will be rejected, with the result that recruiting costs can accumulate to substantial levels simply to maintain a sufficient applicant pool, or positions may remain unfilled for long periods of time. Obviously the answer, if a cutting score is needed, is to set that score somewhere in between these extremes, but where exactly is this happy medium?

A good deal has been written to provide guidance on this matter. Useful sources are an article by Wayne Cascio, Ralph Alexander, and Gerald Barrett in *Personnel Psychology* (1988) and another by Richard Biddle in *Public Personnel Management* (1993). These sources indicate that any approach requires an element of judgment. There is no simple formula that can be applied. In fact, the ideal approach is to avoid using a cutting score at all. This can be achieved

Table 6.1
Judged Employability Levels Derived from Honesty Test Scores

Judged Employability Level	Actual Scores	Standard Scores	Number of Cases (Percent of 70,950)
Extremely high	50-54	80 or above	<1
Very high	45-49	70-79	<1
High	40-44	60-69	15
Above average	35-39	50-59	39
Moderate	30-34	40-49	36
Low	25-29	30-39	5
Very low	20-24	20-29	3
Extremely low	15-19	10-19	1
Not employable	14 or less	0-9	<1

by administering the test to a much larger number of applicants than there are positions to be filled, waiting to make hiring decisions until all applicants have been tested, and then filling the open positions with those who have the highest scores, working down from the top.

This top-down procedure makes the best use of a test's validity. Unfortunately, in many cases, hiring is an ongoing process, with openings continually occurring and selection decisions made without ever building up a large applicant pool; positions cannot be left open long. This is the typical situation in retailing and other contexts where honesty testing is most widely used. Under such circumstances, a resort to cutting scores is inevitable.

Many test publishers provide ready-made cutting scores. These may be established on a simple go–no go or pass-fail basis, or the degree of risk inherent in hiring the person may be specified in terms such as low, moderate, and high risk. In any event, cuts are established to exclude a certain proportion of the people to whom the test has been administered, using the publisher's data base as a reference. Thus, aspects of a particular company's applicant pool are not given attention. Also recognize that it is in a publisher's interest to set as high a cutting score as possible, simply because more tests will have to be administered before a position is filled.

Given these circumstances, it is clearly best for a company to establish its own cutting scores. This does not mean, however, that data from the test publisher cannot provide useful input to this decision. Ideally there will be more than a bare pass-fail designation. Table 6.1 provides an example, using information on a version of the test with which we were involved. The standard scores are not an essential ingredient here, but they do provide some help in interpretation. In this instance, the mean actual score of 35 in the group of 70,950 applicants was set equal to 50, and the standard deviation of 5 was set equal to 10. Thus, the extremely high employability level is four standard deviations above the mean, and the extremely low level four standard deviations below.

The task for a test user is to enter a table similar to Table 6.1 and to establish a cutting score at some point. This point need not be between the categories specified in the table. Thus, if one wanted to exclude at least a third of an applicant pool of essentially the same nature as the 70,950, the cutting score would be set at a standard score of 47. Below that all applicants would be rejected.

In setting cutting scores, several factors have to be considered. One is the base rate for the kinds of behaviors the honesty test is intended to screen out. This base rate can be established in the applicant pool or it may be established for current employees. If the test focuses only on theft, the base rate will be lower than if a wider range of behaviors, including drug and alcohol problems, production deviance, sabotage, and workplace violence, are being targeted. Obviously estimating a base rate is a judgment call, but data of the type discussed in Chapter 1 can be helpful. So too can the opinions of security personnel, human resource managers, and direct supervisors of the positions to be filled using honesty tests. The key point is that the more widespread the behavior is expected to be in a group of applicants, the higher the cutting score should be set. If one expects a base rate of 25 percent, then the cutting score should be set so as to screen out at least that number. Because the tests are not perfect and a margin for error needs to be built in to ensure meeting the base rate, the score selected should, in fact, be one that will screen out more than 25 percent.

A related factor is how crucial it is to eliminate people who might exhibit the targeted behaviors. If the job is one in which opportunities for theft involving large dollar values exist, the situation is quite different from that in which only small amounts can be taken. The higher the cutting score, the more people that will be screened out and thus the less the likelihood that dishonest people will be hired. This argues for setting the cutting score as high as possible, but it also means that a substantial number of honest people will be rejected along with the dishonest. This is a concern that we will consider in more detail shortly.

The most obvious problem, however, is that as more applicants are recruited and then screened to fill a set of openings, hiring costs may skyrocket. In a tight labor market, where applicants are few and hard to attract, it may be almost impossible to maintain a high cutting score and actually fill positions. On the other hand, if people arrive frequently looking for work with a minimum of recruiting effort, there is likely to be no difficulty keeping positions filled even with a high cutting score. Considerations of this kind argue for the use of different cutting scores in different locations and with different jobs. It may even be appropriate to vary the cutting score for a job at the same location with the ebb and flow of the labor force.

The key point is that cutting scores should be set on rational grounds, taking into account costs and benefits of a variety of types. They should be re-evaluated as circumstances change. It should always be possible to state clearly the reasons why the score is where it is at a point in time. This is good selection practice, but it is also desirable from a legal standpoint as well. The courts tend to allow considerable latitude in setting cutting scores, but they do require an approach that seems reasonable.

This discussion focuses on the use of cutting scores with honesty tests. But most of it applies to other types of selection procedures as well. Assuming that several selection procedures (interviews, other tests, and so on) are used by a company, as they should be, and that cutting scores are needed, the points made in this section should have considerable application beyond honesty testing.

DEALING WITH THE FALSE POSITIVE PROBLEM

This problem is a matter of concern for test users in part because it has implications for how test results are reported to applicants, and in part because it has been widely used as an argument against honesty testing. The issue, in one way or another, is related to the frequency (or base rate) of problem behaviors as discussed in Chapter 1, to test validity as discussed in Chapters 3 and 4, and to where the cutting score is set as discussed in the preceding section. Let us start by defining a false positive in the honesty testing context.

Table 3.1 provides the needed data. If a cutting score of 55 on the honesty test is applied to the data of Table 3.1, 37 percent would be eligible for hire and 63 percent would not. This is a relatively high cutting score, but it is consistent with the polygraph results (also considered in the conclusion to Chapter 1). If we then factor in the polygraph results, the exhibit may be summarized as follows:

POLYGRAPH RESULTS

Honesty Test Score	Some Evidence of Dishonesty	No Evidence of Dishonesty
55–69	13	24
20–54	51	12

The people in the upper right and lower left parts of the table are classified in the same manner by both measures. However, 25 percent of the applicants are misclassified. Those in the lower right part of the table are the false positives. They would not be hired based on the honesty test results even though the available evidence from the polygraph suggests they would prove to be honest employees. Thus, the false positive rate is 12 percent.

Obviously, if one wanted to reduce that rate, one way of doing so would be to decrease the cutting score. A decrease of just 5 points to 50 would yield the following result:

POLYGRAPH RESULTS

Honesty Test Score	Some Evidence of Dishonesty	No Evidence of Dishonesty
50–69	26	32
20–49	38	4

Now the false positive rate is only 4 percent, much less of a problem. However, the percent who have test scores making them eligible for hiring, but who nevertheless would prove dishonest based on the polygraph results, has doubled to 26. Now the test is not working well to screen out problem employees. One could decrease the cutting score down to a point in Table 3.1 where there were no false positives, but then the great majority of the dishonest people would be hired, negating the intent of the testing.

False positives present a problem because a number of applicants who would make honest employees are screened out, and not employed, so that a significant portion of those who would present an honesty problem can be screened out as well. The more emotionally charged position is that a large number of individuals who have done nothing wrong, and probably never will, are falsely labeled as thieves and criminals. In this version there is no mention of the other side of the coin—the number of dishonest people hired.

Although there have been other statements on the issue, there is a thread of articles running through the literature that have argued this matter back and forth, pro and con, since 1987. As should be evident by now, conflict-laden issues like this are typical in the honesty testing field. The arguments are complex, and there are points at which we ourselves become confused. We will not attempt to deal with all of this complexity here. However, we do wish to provide some feeling for the nature of the controversy.

The argument began with an article by Kevin Murphy in the *Journal of Applied Psychology* (1987). The major argument in that article is that base rates for problem behavior in the employment situations where honesty tests are used are very low (less than 10 percent) and that consequently false positive rates are typically very high, so high, in fact, that "the debate over the accuracy of these methods is irrelevant" (p. 611). Remember, however, that the base rate in Table 3.1 was not less than 10 percent, but 64 percent.

Next came a series of articles in *The Industrial-Organizational Psychologist*. In the first (February 1989), Philip Manhardt noted that the problems set forth by Murphy apply to all selection procedures, and that to a degree they can compromise much higher base rate levels as well. Thus Murphy is said to introduce what amounts to a superstandard for honesty testing; in applicant selection, where some among many candidates are to be hired in any event, his criteria are too demanding. In a later issue of the same journal (May 1989), Murphy took issue with this position, reiterating his previous statements. Later still (May 1990), Scott Martin and William Terris say, "All else being equal, the false positive rate is simply a function of the validity. A valid predictor, by definition, produces fewer false positive (and false negative) decision errors than a predictor with a lower or zero validity coefficient. . . . If the screening procedure is valid, the proportion of false positives will increase if the procedure is not used for selection" (p. 52).

In the *Journal of Applied Psychology* (1991) Martin and Terris say, "It has been argued, from a social perspective, that valid psychological tests generate too many false-positive decision errors when base rates are low. . . . However, these arguments do not apply to the use of tests for relative decisions, such as those required in personnel selection" (p. 486). Subsequently, in the same journal (1993) Gershon Ben-Shakhar and Maya Bar-Hillel attempt to "rectify the inaccuracies contained in the Martin and Terris (1991) article and to clarify the role of false positives in the evaluation of tests" (p. 148). Dan Dalton, Michael Metzger, and James Wimbush in *Research in Personnel and Human Resource Management* (1994) conclude the debate for the present with an endorsement of the base rate argument as developed by Murphy. For them, the behaviors identified by honesty tests are rare, and thus given what is known about test validities, false positive rates can be assumed to be unacceptably high.

Again, in this debate we find it difficult to sort out pre-existing values from commitments to scientific objectivity. However, a number of distinguished psychologists have come down on the side of the honesty tests. Validity is the governing factor, and to say that false positives are more important in honesty testing is to introduce special standards for these tests alone. This is the position taken in the American Psychological Association review and in the meta-analytic review article by Deniz Ones, Chockalingam Viswesvaran, and Frank Schmidt (1993). Paul Sackett, Laura Burris, and Christine Callahan take a similar position in their review article in *Personnel Psychology* (1989) as well.

In *Current Directions in Psychological Science* (1994) Paul Sackett had the following to say:

An important aspect of the misclassification issue is that misclassification rates are interpretable only in comparison with alternatives. A test that misclassifies, say 25% of test takers may prove dismal, or it may prove a great improvement over available alternatives.

A good example of the failure to apply this form of analysis to the misclassification problem can be found in comments made by Senator Edward Kennedy during debate about the Employee Polygraph Protection Act. Kennedy noted that even if one accepts the claims of polygraph proponents that polygraph examinations have an accuracy rate of 95%, if 1 million preemployment polygraph exams are administered annually, a 5% error rate means that 50,000 innocent job applicants are misclassified. Kennedy argued that any device that misclassifies 50,000 people per year should be banned. This argument reduces all personnel selection to the absurd, in that all selection devices, from tests to interviews, are certainly less than perfectly accurate, and thus should be banned by Kennedy's standard. Yet the alternative—random selection or first-come, first-served—results in higher rates of misclassification than any selection device with nonzero validity. (pp. 75–76)

An article by Scott Martin in the *Journal of Business and Psychology* (1990) illustrates this point by comparing false positive rates under random selection with those for honesty tests, selection interviews, and weighted application blanks. Random selection is obviously the least valid, followed in ascending order by selection interviews, the application blank, and the honesty test, with the honesty test being most valid. Holding the cutting score at the same point, with the base rate for theft at 16 percent, the false positive rates were 34, 25, 20, and 14 percent, respectively. If the base rate is moved to 48 percent, very close to the 50 percent that would minimize the false positive rate, the figures are 26, 19, 15, and 10 percent. Clearly the base rate makes a difference, but validity matters more.

Much of the argument for the influence of low base rates and high false positive rates is predicated on the assumption that theft is rare in most employment contexts. Certainly there are jobs where this is true; there are even some jobs in which all the types of behaviors that honesty tests measure are rare. But to use detected theft as an index for base rates can be very misleading. A large amount of theft goes undetected, and honesty tests measure a great deal more than theft. Furthermore, honesty tests are used for jobs where there is substantial opportunity for theft, and where other types of problem behaviors are high as well. The false positive issue arose from a claim of a base rate below 10 percent. Honesty tests are very unlikely to be used in that context. From the data of Chapter 1 it is apparent that most employers using honesty tests have an applicant pool where the base rate for dishonesty ranges from 33 percent to 67 percent. The false positive issue is less significant under these circumstances, although it does not disappear.

Scott Martin, again writing in the *Journal of Business and Psychology* (1989), proposes that the false positive rate can also be reduced by having a group of applicants who were below the cutting score initially take another test (perhaps a personality-based measure, subsequent to an initial overt integrity test). Those who do poorly on both tests can be assumed to represent poor risks. Those who do well the second time are more likely to have been false positives on the first test. To the extent the two tests differ and both are valid, overall validity of selection increases. This is another argument for using two independent honesty tests, with different factor structures, in a selection battery.

A major concern raised in the Office of Technology Assessment review, and by others, is that those who are false positives will be labeled as dishonest unfairly and perhaps stigmatized for years. This is used as a major argument for holding honesty tests to a higher standard than other selection procedures. Even if one does not accept the idea that a superstandard should be applied to honesty testing, the prospect that a number of people will be falsely labeled should be a source of concern for an employer. It is not humane, and it is not the way to create goodwill for a company in the marketplace and the labor force either.

Given this, we recommend that companies do what many indeed already do, and simply avoid any possibility of labeling and stigma. All applicants will have at a very minimum an employment interview and an application form to fill out, in addition to the honesty testing. There is no need to provide specific feedback on which selection procedure(s) contributed to the decision against hiring. It may well be that there were simply better qualified people available. A statement to the effect that the company was able to locate someone who more closely matched company needs is really all that is required. Most of us are turned down for employment at one time or another in our lives, often many times. There is no special stigma involved. Not hiring an applicant based in part or wholly on honesty test results is very different from firing an employee from a job, in which he or she may have certain vested rights. On occasion these two situations are set equal to one another as the conflict over honesty testing escalates. We do not find this type of argument persuasive.

TRAINING TEST USERS

A number of test publishers make available training programs of various kinds to teach company personnel about honesty testing in general and about their particular tests. These programs can last from a few hours to several days. They may be focused on managers whose staffing practices are influenced by honesty tests or on those who will administer the tests.

John Jones and Joseph Orban describe a brief program of the former type in a *Journal of Business and Psychology* article (1992). Topics include:

1. Documenting the business necessity of honesty tests.
2. Understanding the strengths and limitations of honesty tests.
3. Reviewing industry-specific validation and adverse impact studies.
4. Integrating an honesty test into an overall human resource selection program.
5. Protecting job applicant's privacy rights.
6. Understanding the *Uniform Guidelines* issued by the federal Equal Employment Opportunity Commission.
7. Following the Association of Personnel Test Publisher's Model Guidelines.
8. Upgrading recruitment methods.

The program usually considers the specific honesty test involved, dealing with what it measures and what results are expected of it. There will be discussions of how the test is administered and scored, and how to deal with questions that applicants may raise. Much of the training material typically derives from the publisher's test manual, and in fact trainees are often provided with a copy of the manual which they read during training.

Much the same material is covered in training programs for test administrators. However, there is also consideration of the physical testing environment, test instructions, the mechanics of test scoring, test security issues, and the handling of special problems that may arise. Although often neglected, the setting and use of cutting scores should be given particular attention.

The extent to which formal classroom training is required depends on the professional training of company personnel. Reading the test manual may be sufficient. Often training covers what is in the present book, although in less detail. Some publishers pressure users into formal training to foster a closer tie between publisher and user. It is important that a test publisher have a training program available in any event. Exactly how and with whom a company should utilize this training should be adjusted to the particular situation. In dealing with some issues, it may be desirable to have company personnel or independent consultants become involved.

IDENTIFYING BARRIERS TO TESTING

We strongly suggest that all serious candidates for a job where honesty considerations are relevant be tested if at all possible—at least with one honesty test and quite possibly with two. There are certain legal factors involved here which we will take up in the next chapter, but testing everyone is desirable from the standpoint of good selection practice. It is not unheard of for companies to reject certain applicants early, before testing occurs, on the grounds that these people do not appear to be the kind the company employs, or perhaps based on the judgment that an individual looks dishonest. These judgments can be highly unreliable, varying depending on who does the judging, and they can be just plain wrong.

One barrier to testing all candidates may be that the applicant's primary language is not English. If the job does not require English language fluency, this can cause the honesty test to become an inappropriate hurdle based on considerations that have nothing to do with honesty at all. Some honesty tests are available in other languages, particularly Spanish. If a test is under serious consideration, inquiries should be made regarding other language editions, or perhaps a translation can be prepared. What we do not recommend is that a test which on other grounds appears unsatisfactory be adopted simply because it is available in languages other than English. Rather than do this, it would be preferable to have a test administered orally by an interpreter. Ideally other language editions should be validated separately in the context in which they will be used.

A second barrier to testing is literacy. At the extreme it may be necessary to resort to oral administration. In general, if the applicant has completed a year or so of high school, effects of educational level on honesty test scores are unlikely. Our data in this regard are given in Table 4.1.

Approaches exist that may be applied to text materials to establish the grade level at which the test is written. In the case of the test with which we worked, the test was at a seventh grade reading level, indicating that a person who reads at the seventh grade level should be able to understand all segments of the test. Other tests may require a somewhat higher level of reading comprehension. This is particularly likely to become a problem in the introductory instructional materials. On occasion, the questions themselves appear to have been written at a relatively low reading level. Yet when it comes to introducing the test and explaining how to complete it, this limitation may be relaxed.

Most test publishers provide readability information, or will if asked. However, we believe there is no substitute for actual experience administering a test to applicants with relatively low educational attainment. If a person shows evidence of struggling, ask him or her to read you some of the questions. Often those whose literacy is marginal for a test will take much longer to complete it than most other test-takers.

Where barriers to completing a test introduced by language and literacy considerations are operating, a special scale may be very useful in identifying the problem. If people do not understand the questions, they may guess at their meanings. This is likely to produce many responses of the kind obtained when a random response pattern is adopted. A special scale made up of high-frequency answers is likely to identify those with language or literacy problems at its low end; these people do not understand the high-frequency, socially desirable answers well enough to select them. Similarly, a scale consisting of rare or unusual answers should yield a high score among these individuals because they are forced to guess at meanings and often are in error. In instances of this type a second administration will not solve the problem. The only way the test can be administered is orally or perhaps using an audio tape. When a large number of questions are skipped, that, too, may reflect language or literacy problems. Again, oral administration or an audio tape become necessary.

Clearly, oral testing on any large scale drives the cost of testing up substantially. There are situations where the nature of the applicant pool introduces so many barriers to testing that it is not cost-effective to use honesty tests. This is unfortunate, but it is also realistic. Users should not try to use the tests when language and literacy barriers appear to be affecting a large proportion of test scores.

CONCLUSIONS

In this chapter we have discussed a number of issues that should be the primary responsibility of test users. Validity, reliability, question types, test dimensions, and susceptibility to faking are inherent in tests and are introduced by those who create them. From a user perspective, these factors are important in making decisions about what test to use and which test publisher to employ. However, there is little the user can do to actually change these aspects of the test once an adoption decision is made. The considerations treated here, on the other hand, can be handled in different ways by the users of the tests, and how they are handled makes a difference in the effectiveness of the testing program.

Cutting scores, if necessary, should be established by the user, not the publisher, taking into account information the publisher can provide, but adding in data on recruiting costs, tightness of the labor market, base rates, and the like that come from other sources. There needs to be a solid rationale behind the score that is selected. If a top-down strategy can be used, rather than a cutting score, it should be.

To the extent feasible, without compromising validity, false positive rates should be minimized. This should not extend to setting cutting scores so low that the honesty tests do not achieve their purpose, however. The use of two uncorrelated, or minimally correlated, honesty tests administered at the same time as part of a test battery can provide both more effective prediction and a way to reduce the number of false positives. Testing costs will be higher, but the benefits would seem to warrant the cost. Getting two test publishers involved may have benefits on other grounds as well. Also, the negative effects of false positives can be held down by avoiding any attribution of dishonesty to those who are not hired; you should not tell people that they failed the honesty test.

Training programs related to honesty testing may or may not be required, but some procedure for informing the managers who will be affected by the testing should be adopted. It is important as well to be sure that test administrators are knowledgeable about the tests and capable of handling any problems that might arise. Input from test publishers to training programs is desirable, and users should avail themselves of the information publishers have to offer. However, we do not believe that the information provided to interested parties should be limited to publisher sources.

There are many considerations regarding the company itself, honesty problems the company has faced, the decision to adopt a test, validity in the local context, local labor force characteristics, and even the principles of effective psychological testing (and honesty testing) that are best handled from sources other than the test publisher. Depending on the issue and the circumstances, these sources might be people on the company staff or outside consultants. In general, we believe companies should design their own training programs, and then integrate test publisher inputs into the framework thus established.

Finally, companies are in a position to determine who will and will not be tested. There are very good reasons for testing all job applicants. However, if there is reason to place honesty testing late in the screening process after a number of applicants have been rejected on other grounds, well-established procedures should be devised for sequencing selection components. Avoiding off-the-cuff prior judgments about applicants that might in some cases, but not others, replace the honesty testing is particularly important.

Barriers to testing created by language factors and literacy considerations present a special challenge. Much testing is done with applicant pools that do not introduce these kinds of problems, or do so only rarely. However, there are situations where large numbers of applicants are not fluent in English or have literacy deficiencies. Solutions may involve translations, reducing reading levels (especially of instructions), or using audio tapes or oral administrations, depending on the source of the problem. At the extreme these barriers may be so frequent in a particular applicant group that honesty tests should not be used. In any event, it is essential to avoid having a person fail to achieve the cutting score not because of dishonesty, but because of language or literacy problems. This is a type of false positive that can be avoided.

In summary, there are a number of features of an honesty testing program that should not, and in some cases really cannot, be left to the test publishers. Some publishers make it a practice to try to do as much as possible for their customers so that honesty testing is a minimal burden on them. The result, however, can be that some things that should be done do not get done, and others are not carried out in a way that fits well with local circumstances. An effective honesty testing program is a joint effort, with certain activities clearly allocated to the publisher and other activities clearly retained by the company. We have tried in this chapter to provide information regarding how this division of labor might best occur.

7

Honesty Testing and the Law: Employment Discrimination

Like any other selection procedure, honesty tests have a potential for discrimination in the employment process. If companies run the risk of legal action by using the tests, this is good reason for steering clear of honesty tests. We need, therefore, to take a close look at discrimination law, and how honesty tests fare relative to this law.

EQUAL EMPLOYMENT OPPORTUNITY LAW OVER THE FIRST 25 YEARS

Hiring is the area of human resource activity that has experienced the greatest legal impact since the mid-1960s. Prior to the enactment of fair employment legislation, employers were largely free to select anyone they wanted as employees. Most legal influences on human resources involved the employment relationship with those already on the payroll. This situation changed drastically, however. The major influences came from laws (at the local, state, and federal levels) prohibiting discrimination in employment because of race, sex, or age.

There now are more than 25 federal laws and executive orders that speak to one aspect or another of equal employment opportunity. The first such statute was enacted by New York State in 1945, and over the next 20 years, half the other states followed suit. The biggest impetus to equal opportunity in employment, however, came with the passage of the Civil Rights Act of 1964, Title VII of which prohibits discrimination in employment based on race, color, religion, national origin, or sex. The law applies to employers, labor unions, and employment agencies. In the years during which this Civil Rights Act has been in operation, the number of complaints of job discrimination has grown steadily.

Title VII is enforced by the Equal Employment Opportunity Commission

(EEOC). Under the original law, the EEOC tried to effect compliance by conferences with the parties involved, conciliation, and persuasion. If these efforts failed, the EEOC could ask the attorney general to bring a civil suit against the employer. These enforcement procedures proved to be slow and cumbersome, and they resulted in the passage of amendments to the Act in 1972, giving EEOC the power to bring enforcement actions directly through the federal courts. The commission continues to attempt to push enforcement of equal opportunity through the use of conciliation agreements and consent decrees; however, the fact that EEOC now can go directly to court and has won settlements that require paying large amounts of back compensation adds considerable clout in enforcing the law. The EEOC may take a charge of discrimination brought to it and file suit in federal district court. The EEOC also may decline to take a case and issue a right-to-sue letter; this letter permits plaintiffs to take cases to court on their own.

Executive orders that apply to government contractors are another option available to the federal government for policing employment discrimination. Such orders date back to World War II, but the one that has had the most significant impact is Order No. 11246, issued in 1965. That order not only prohibits government contractors from discrimination in employment but also requires that they take ''affirmative action'' to make sure that such discrimination does not exist. The order is implemented by the Office of Federal Contract Compliance Programs (OFCCP) in the U.S. Department of Labor, which has authority to terminate contracts and to debar companies from bidding on government contracts in the future.

Both EEOC and OFCCP originally issued detailed guidelines related to the use of tests and testing procedures. These subsequently were combined into a single set of Uniform Guidelines on Employee Selection Procedures. This concern with tests was anticipated by various members of Congress when the Civil Rights Act of 1964 was passed, and Title VII includes a provision indicating that testing for selection purposes is legal as long as the test is not specifically designed, intended, or used to discriminate. The provision was added as an outgrowth of a case in the early 1960s in which the Illinois Fair Employment Practices Commission questioned the use of a standard verbal ability test by the Motorola Company.

Despite this provision in the law, the crucial issue in the use of tests and other hiring practices, according to the U.S. Supreme Court, is not the employer's intent but the result. If the practice results in discrimination against a protected group, and cannot be shown to be related to job performance, then the practice is prohibited. The significance of this ruling for employers is that they must be able to show that tests and other hiring procedures are proven measures of job performance. In the Court's words, ''What Congress has commanded is that any tests used must measure the person for the job and not the person in the abstract.'' This position is set forth in the pivotal *Griggs v. Duke Power Company* case described below.

Under the Title VII of the Civil Rights Act, unlawful discrimination means:

1. to fail or refuse to hire or to discharge any individual, or otherwise to discriminate against any individual with respect to compensation, terms, conditions, or privileges of employment, because of such individual's race, color, religion, sex, or national origin; or
2. to limit, segregate, or classify employees or applicants for employment in any way which would deprive or tend to deprive any individual of employment opportunities or otherwise adversely affect his or her status as an employee, because of such individual's race, color, religion, sex, or national origin.

Duke Power Company employed 95 people in its Dan River Steam Station in Draper, North Carolina, 14 of whom were black. For many years the company had restricted black employees to low-paying, unskilled jobs in the labor department and had required a high school diploma for promotion out of the department. With the passage of the Civil Rights Act, the company introduced an additional requirement that no one could be promoted out of the labor department without obtaining satisfactory scores on the Wonderlic Personnel Test and the Bennett Mechanical Comprehension Test. No evidence was developed by the company to show that these tests had a relationship to job performance— that high scorers performed well or low scorers poorly. Furthermore, it was immediately evident that very few blacks in the labor department could pass the tests, whereas most whites could. Thus blacks remained essentially barred from promotion to the more desirable and higher paying jobs.

In reviewing this situation, the Supreme Court of the United States came to the following conclusions:

The Civil Rights Act proscribes not only discrimination but also practices that are fair in form, but discriminatory in operation. The touchstone is business necessity. If an employment practice which operates to exclude Negroes cannot be shown to be related to job performance, the practice is prohibited. . . . Good intent or absence of discriminatory intent does not redeem employment procedures or testing mechanisms that operate as ''built-in headwinds'' for minority groups and are unrelated to measuring job capability.

In *Griggs v. Duke Power Company* the Court found, with regard to the high school graduation requirement and the need to pass the two tests of intelligence and mechanical ability, that:

1. neither standard is shown to be significantly related to successful job performance;
2. both requirements operate to disqualify Negroes at a substantially higher rate than white applicants; and

3. the job in question formerly had been filled only by white employees as part of a long-standing practice of giving preference to whites.

The standards and tests to be used should measure the person for the job and not the person in the abstract. At Duke Power this requirement was not met and, as a result, the company was found guilty of illegal discrimination by the Supreme Court.

The inclusion of sex as a basis of discrimination to be prohibited by Title VII of the Civil Rights Act was an effort to defeat the bill at the time it was passed; its inclusion was even opposed by the Women's Bureau of the U.S. Department of Labor. The interpretation of this provision has proved to be one of the most difficult problems for the EEOC, as it has faced an increasing number of sex discrimination complaints over the years.

One basis for the difficulties in enforcing the ban on sex discrimination in employment is that such discrimination may be permissible where sex is a bona fide occupational qualification (BFOQ), necessary to the employer's normal operation. The BFOQ exception also applies to discrimination based on religion or nationality, but not to racial discrimination. What constitutes a BFOQ has been subject to different interpretations in various courts, although the EEOC itself maintains that this exception should be interpreted narrowly. Jobs may be restricted to one sex for reasons of authenticity (as, for example, actresses or models portraying women) or on the basis of community standards of morality or propriety (as in the case of restroom attendants), but not on the basis of general assumptions of characteristics or stereotypes of men or women in general.

There were some proposals to provide protection for older workers under the Civil Rights Act of 1964, but in the end, age was not included as one of the bases of job discrimination prohibited by Title VII. Three years later, however, Congress enacted the Age Discrimination in Employment Act of 1967, providing many of the same strictures against discrimination in employment for persons aged 40 to 65 that Title VII provided with respect to race, sex, religion, and national origin. There are certain exceptions for bona fide occupational qualifications based on age. The Age Discrimination Act is now enforced by the EEOC and has been extended to cover older persons without any upper age limit. The Older Workers Benefit Protection Act was passed in 1990 to clarify the status of employee benefit plans under the law and to ensure that the benefits of older workers equal those of workers who are younger.

The initial enforcement of the Age Discrimination Act was aimed at reducing the number of newspaper advertisements for job vacancies that list a maximum age or use terms such as "young person" or "recent college graduate." More recently, the government, going to court on behalf of older workers who were forced into early retirement or separation, has succeeded in getting some of these workers reinstated in their jobs and in obtaining substantial amounts of back pay for them; cases of this type are increasing. In general, the courts have been most sympathetic to the discrimination claims of those in the protected group who are in fact older; people in their forties are unlikely to win such a case.

Over the years, the courts—including the U.S. Supreme Court—have changed positions several times on what constitutes discrimination. The implications for selection and placement have been pronounced. At the present time, selection procedures such as honesty tests face no problems if they do not produce adverse impact—that is, contribute to the hiring of one group more frequently than another. Even if there is adverse impact, however, this does not constitute discrimination if it can be shown that the selection procedure is related to job performance. This business necessity defense relies on the fact that a selection procedure can be shown to be job-related. The appropriate way to demonstrate this job relatedness is to conduct some type of validation showing that the selection procedure actually measures what it is supposed to measure: the level of job performance or some other job-related factor, such as turnover rate.

For honesty tests, this means applying one or more of the validation procedures discussed in Chapter 3—the more the better. An additional approach, considered in the enforcement agency guidelines, is called content validation. This type of validity is based on systematic study of the particular job to learn the knowledge, skills, and behaviors required to perform it. If honesty considerations are pronounced in such a job analysis, and they are clearly manifested in a test, then an argument for content validity would seem warranted. This would typically be true of most clear-purpose or overt tests, but seems less likely for personality-based or disguised-purpose tests.

We know of no honesty test case in which content validity has been relied upon in connection with a business necessity defense. A reading of court cases in general suggests that using content validity alone as a legal defense is risky. Judges tend to find the concept a difficult one, and opinions dealing with it have varied considerably. We believe, therefore, that content validity arguments should be used primarily as supplements to arguments based on criterion-related research.

A final point is the determination of how much adverse impact is too much—triggering the need to do some type of validation. Say an honesty test causes more whites than blacks to exceed the cutting score and qualify for employment. How large does this difference have to be before it is viewed as indicating possible discrimination?

Four possible answers to this question are indicated by James Ledvinka and Vida Scarpello in their book *Federal Regulation of Personnel and Human Resource Management* (1991).

1. The difference is large enough so that it offends a judge's subjective notion of fairness.

2. The difference is large enough so that it violates the four-fifths rule; i.e., the proportion qualifying for employment in the discriminated-against group is less than four-fifths (or 80 percent) of the proportion in the majority group. This is the standard promulgated by federal EEO agencies; it has on occasion been adopted by the courts.

3. The difference is large enough that, statistically speaking, it would not be expected to occur by chance alone more than 5 percent of the time; i.e., the probability level is below 0.05 ($p < 0.05$).

4. The difference is large enough that the proportions selected in the two groups differ from one another by more than two, or sometimes three, standard deviations.

Ideally, a company will operate its selection system so as not to run afoul of any of these criteria of possible discrimination. Note that statistical analyses can play an important role here, just as they do in validation.

HOW HONESTY TESTS STACK UP IN TERMS OF ADVERSE IMPACT

A considerable body of research deals with the potential for adverse impact inherent in various honesty tests. Most of these studies follow points 2 and 3 above. They apply the four-fifths rule and/or they look at the statistical significance of the difference in proportions deemed hirable in the two groups. The goal for the publishers is to present evidence that two groups, say blacks and whites, do not differ. A number of studies also consider the differences between mean test scores for the groups. If the mean honesty test score of the blacks tested, for instance, does not differ statistically ($p < 0.05$) from the mean for the whites, that is presumed to be evidence for a lack of adverse impact.

Based on these kinds of analyses, it is widely reported that adverse impact is rarely if ever produced by honesty tests. Thus, Paul Sackett, writing in *Current Directions in Psychological Science* (1994), says:

There has been extensive documentation that women, racial minority groups, and older workers do not systematically perform more poorly than other groups on these tests, and thus there have been no successful challenges to integrity tests under federal antidiscrimination law. (pp. 74–75)

We agree with this conclusion. However, we believe it is important to add several points. A major reason why differences are not found is that items that might produce adverse impact are often deleted in the process of test development. Michael Cunningham and Philip Ash discuss this process in their *Journal of Business and Psychology* article (1988). Thus, the findings reported for many tests say little about the real differences in honesty existing in the population.

In spite of this procedure, however, differences in test scores in favor of females and older workers are found with sufficient frequency to provide convincing evidence of differences. These findings appear to be consistent with actual behavior at work based on the data Richard Hollinger and John Clark present in *Theft by Employees* (1983). Nevertheless, they can provide evidence supporting a charge of reverse discrimination against males and younger employees.

Let us look at some actual examples. M. J. Riley, writing in *Central State Business Review* (1982), reports a study in which 250 people who completed an honesty test were classified as high, medium, or low risk. In the age analysis, test-takers below 27 years old were found to concentrate significantly more heavily in the high-risk category. This is consistent with other findings that it is the applicant in the mid-20s or younger who is particularly likely to do poorly on honesty tests, and to exhibit more problem behavior on the job as well.

Judith Tansky and Marjorie Armstrong-Stassen, writing in the *Southern Management Association Proceedings* (1995) and in an additional working paper (1996), describe research carried out in university settings where male and female students were compared. Two commercially marketed honesty tests were used. The females consistently obtained scores indicative of greater honesty, across tests and across several different samples.

We also have data from our own research. Scored in the usual way, separate keys are used with different race and sex groups, and these results are set equal to each other so that adverse impact is not present. However, at one point we developed a single scale which could be used with everybody. Using this scale, comparisons among groups can be made quite legitimately.

We selected representative groups of 100 from our larger job applicant data base for this purpose. Higher scores indicate greater honesty. The mean scores were as follows:

Black females	36.3
Hispanic females	35.4
Black males	35.1
White females	35.0
Hispanic males	34.6
White males	34.0

These differences are not large, but they are statistically significant. The white males score at a relatively low level. They are least likely to do well on the test.

We also looked at the results obtained when the four-fifths rule is invoked. From the more than 70,000 cases in the data base, we calculated the proportion the white male selection ratio is of the selection ratio for all others, using various cutting scores. The results are contained in Table 7.1. Between scores of 34 and 35 the four-fifths rule begins to be violated. Thus, the cutting score can be set at a level low enough so that no adverse impact will occur. Doing this means that roughly a third of all applicants will be screened out.

Table 7.1 is particularly important because it demonstrates that where a cutting score is set can determine whether the four-fifths rule is violated. If there is reason to believe a test may be viewed as operating to produce discrimination,

Table 7.1
How Cutting Scores Relate to the Four-Fifths Rule

If all individuals with this score or above are hired--	The selection ratio for white males will be this percent of the selection ratio for all others--
Dishonest end	
30	95
31	93
32	92
33	88
34	82
35	76
36	70
37	64
38	62
39	60
40	59
Honest end	

it is worth determining whether changing the cutting score will eliminate this concern.

This example involves the reverse discrimination situation where males, or younger people, do less well on the test. This is not what fair employment legislation was intended to correct. The laws were introduced to reduce discrimination against certain protected groups—blacks, females, older people. Can reverse discrimination cases be brought and won under the law? Perhaps, as David Twomey demonstrates in his book *Equal Employment Opportunity Law* (1994). In one instance a white male employee of the federal Equal Employment Opportunity Commission won just such a case against that agency. However, the risk for an organization of being found guilty of reverse discrimination is relatively low. Such cases are rare, and plaintiffs will find winning them difficult, simply because they do not conform to the primary intent of the law.

ADVERSE IMPACT IN COMPANY HIRING

The kinds of studies discussed in the previous section are useful to employers because they can serve to show that adverse impact is unlikely. Selecting a test that research has indicated is free of bias against protected groups is evidence of a good faith effort to avoid discrimination. However, it does not guarantee against a finding of adverse impact. The legal definition of adverse impact has to do with the setting and conditions where a test is actually used. Thus, there can be variations from one company to another, and even from one company location to another. It is what happens at the point of hiring that matters.

Let us take a hypothetical example from our own experience to illustrate what can happen. In this instance, we used the test as scored separately with special scales for each race and sex group. The scores from each such scale were then combined by setting each mean at 50 and each standard deviation at 10. Thus in the normative sample there could be no adverse impact. In a particular company situation, the cutting score was set so that scores of 50 or below caused a person to be rejected and scores of 51 or higher lead to hiring.

In this context, 64 percent of all white male applicants were hired. The percentages for all three other groups were below this figure. To apply the four-fifths rule, the proportions of the white male selection ratio achieved in the other groups were calculated:

Black females	0.80
Black males	0.79
White females	0.66

Irrespective of the particular basis for the complaint, this is not an attractive picture. All three protected groups were well below the white males in the extent to which hiring occurred. For the black females and black males, using the four-fifths rule, the figures were marginal, but the white female figure was clearly unacceptable. Given the overall picture, a judge could well view discrimination as likely in all three protected groups.

How can adverse impact of this kind occur when on other grounds there is little evidence to support a charge of discrimination? One answer to this problem is provided by Dan Dalton, Michael Metzger, and James Wimbush in their *Research in Personnel and Human Resources Management* article (1994):

That mean test scores on some indicator do not differ by protected group is one thing. That different cut-scores may be used by some integrity test users as a function of who (i.e., members of what group) receives the scores is a different matter altogether. (p. 145)

They then go on to describe a hypothetical situation where a test publisher designates a job candidate as marginal. There is nothing to worry about if the company consistently does not hire such marginal candidates and if no difference exists in the proportion from protected groups who receive the marginal label. There is a problem, however, if the decision regarding hiring is based on considerations which do influence protected candidates. For example, a company might give a special chance to candidates of one race who were marginal, but not to candidates of another race. This would amount to a differential cut-off score.

It is also possible that a company may attract a disproportionately large number of highly qualified white males to its applicant pool in the first place, perhaps because it has the reputation of being a good place for white males to work. The honesty test selects more white males simply because the recruiting process predisposes to this result. This recruiting process might discourage white females from applying, with the consequence that fewer qualified females are considered.

There are other possible reasons for this type of result. The important point, however, is that adverse impact is established at the point of actual hiring and rejection. It can reflect intentional discrimination, but more likely it occurs unintentionally as a consequence of factors not recognized as having any influence on the outcome.

IMPACT OF THE CIVIL RIGHTS ACT OF 1991

The following quote from an article in *HR Focus* (1992) written by John Cook, an attorney specializing in employment law, points up the uncertainties introduced by the Civil Rights Act of 1991, the most recent piece of legislation dealing with discrimination.

The compromise that ended the legislative debate over hiring quotas long enough to allow passage of the 1991 Civil Rights Act was one in which both sides declared victory. The heart of the compromise was the enactment of vague and ambiguous language, the meaning of which is being hotly contested. In essence, Congress agreed to disagree and left the resolution of this critically important social issue to the courts. One thing already is clear: the Civil Rights Act will require all employers to track and maintain statistics and documentation in a manner that only the largest and most sophisticated employers have done in the past. Without these critical data, employers often may face no-win litigation. (p. 12)

There is general agreement that the ambiguities inherent in the law mean that it will be a number of years before its true meaning becomes clear.

Although diverse in its coverage, the act's primary purpose is to reverse a number of Supreme Court decisions since *Griggs v. Duke Power Company* that made it easier for companies to defend against a charge of discrimination. Thus, the law served to relax the burden of proof in bringing equal employment opportunity claims and returned to the types of criteria enunciated in the Griggs case.

Among other provisions, the law expands granting compensatory and punitive damages and use of jury trials, places restrictions on the ways that psychological test scores are used, introduces stipulations regarding EEOC activities, and extends the rights of government employees. A special commission was established to study limitations on the promotion of protected group members such as women and blacks. The law is not so much a proactive document as a reaction to recent Supreme Court decisions and to perceived inconsistencies and loopholes in previous equal employment opportunity legislation.

One loophole was that existing law permitted separately norming the test scores of various groups so that, for instance, whites would only be compared with other whites and blacks with other blacks. This way, if one group scored higher than the other overall, that difference would be eliminated. Whereas a single normative distribution might result in fewer members of a protected group being hired, separate norming would serve to introduce equality, and thus eliminate adverse impact. In the process reverse discrimination could occur as lower scoring members of a protected group come to replace higher scoring members of a non-protected group in a company's hiring priorities.

To close this loophole, the Civil Rights Act of 1991 included the following wording:

It shall be an unlawful employment practice for a respondent, in connection with the selection or referral of applicants as candidates for employment or promotion, to adjust the scores of, use different cutoff scores for, or otherwise alter the results of, employment related tests on the basis of race, color, religion, sex, or national origin.

This requirement can have significant implications for honesty testing, although there is good reason to believe that this was not its intent. The chief objective was to eliminate separate norming by subgroups when the General Aptitude Test Battery (GATB), developed by the U.S. Employment Service, is used in employment offices throughout the country. The GATB is a multi-measure index of general or mental abilities, and like most such measures, it yields higher scores on the average for whites than blacks. To remove this effect, the Employment Service introduced subgroup norming. However, this practice came under attack as reverse discrimination. Congress agreed with that contention and introduced specific wording to eliminate the practice. A book entitled *Fairness in Employment Testing: Validity Generalization, Minority Issues, and the General Aptitude Test Battery* (1989) by John Hartigan and Alexandra Wigdor and a follow-on paper by Alexandra Wigdor and Paul Sackett published in the edited volume *Personnel Selection and Assessment: Individual and Organizational Perspectives* (1993) provide details on the use of subgroup norming with the GATB.

Like other aspects of the 1991 act, it is not clear exactly what Congress said when it passed the prohibition on subgroup norming. It is clear what was intended insofar as tests like the GATB are concerned. Beyond that, however, uncertainty abounds. It appears that the impact on personality measures such as honesty tests was not even considered. A good discussion of practices that may or may not be proscribed is contained in a report by the Scientific Affairs Committee of the Society for Industrial and Organizational Psychology, printed in *The Industrial-Organizational Psychologist* (1993).

As has been our practice, we will use our experience with the test on which we collaborated to illustrate how the 1991 law affected honesty testing. Although our particular situation differed in several respects from that of a number of other honesty tests, it was not unique. An article by Hilary Knatz, Robin

Inwald, Albert Brockwell, and Linh Tran in the *Journal of Business and Psychology* (1992), for instance, deals with similar issues involving a different test.

In the late 1980s we requested a legal opinion regarding our test's status under federal law. This is what we received:

[Y]our test . . . has been designed in accordance with generally accepted professional and scientific standards so as to produce results which do not differentiate among respondents based upon whether they are male, female, black, or white. We understand that any test-related variation characteristic of one or another of those groups or combinations of such groups has been eliminated through the method by which scoring has been consolidated into a uniform scale. Against this background, we conclude that Title VII of the Civil Rights Act of 1964 does not prohibit the use of [the test] with respect to such groups. We further conclude that such use of [the test] is not prohibited by the federal Uniform Guidelines on Employee Selection Procedures or by equal employment requirements applying to employers holding federal contracts or subcontracts.

This gave us no cause for concern, and we proceeded to market the test widely. Yet in 1991, as the new law went into effect, another completely different opinion solicited by our employer from the company's law firm brought our marketing to a halt:

[I]n light of the race norming provision of the recently enacted 1991 Civil Rights Act, it would be prudent to advise the users of [the test] of the Act's likely prohibitive effect on the continued use of [the test]. In particular, they should be advised that as of the effective date of the Act, any administration or use of [the test] in the employment selection process may be a violation of the Act. They should be advised to consider no further use of [the test] until further notice from the Company.

This triggered a frantic effort to put the test in conformance with the new law, or at least with what we thought the new law was. As originally developed the scoring keys were quite different for the four race and sex groups (see Chapter 5). The scoring key for each group was created so as to maximize validity for that group; then the disparate scores were put on a common scale by setting each group mean equal to 50 and each group standard deviation equal to 10. This produced a result tantamount to subgroup norming, but done for the purpose of obtaining maximum validity.

The new all-purpose, or undifferentiated, scoring system used the existing 82 items and produced a scale employing those particular items that distinguish honest from dishonest people (based on the polygraph results) without reference to race or sex. Findings based on the resulting procedure are contrasted with those from the original one in Table 7.2. On all counts the new approach falls short of its predecessor. It is less valid, less reliable, has fewer scorable items, differentiates less effectively, and makes much less use of the scenario items for which we had so much hope in the beginning. The new approach is not bad;

Table 7.2
The Original Scoring Differentiated by Sex and Race Compared with the New Undifferentiated Scoring

	Differentiated Scoring	Undifferentiated Scoring
Validity	0.69	0.62
Reliability	0.98	0.80
Scorable Items (of 82)	77	41
Possible Score Range	135	79
% of Items With a Weight Above 1	73	17
% of Scenario Items Scored	91	28
% of Confession and Honesty Attitude Items Scored	100	93
Correlation Between the Scores Derived from the Two Systems	0.74	

it is just less good. The only argument that can be made in favor of the new scoring is that it may be generalizable beyond blacks and whites.

We present this example to show what to consider if the Civil Rights Act of 1991 becomes an issue in selecting an honesty test. After the law was passed, there was hope that the EEOC would clarify some of the ambiguities, and perhaps even specify whether personality, and honesty, tests were covered, in addition to tests of mental ability. Yet, for five years now there has been only silence. We are sure that the law firm that rendered the 1991 opinion would recommend today the same as it did before. More and more it seems that "the baby was indeed thrown out with the bath water."

Another point that emerges from this example is that the confession and honesty attitude items yield scores that are much the same (correlating around 0.82) among the protected groups—white females, black females, and black males; on these same items the white males remain close to the other groups, but to a lesser extent, with correlations around 0.62—some 0.20 points lower. But on the scenario items major disparities appear. Black males and females still score somewhat alike (correlating at about 0.50). Whites simply are not like blacks at all, however, and white males and females are distinctly unalike (the correlation is −0.45).

We conclude that major race and sex differences exist in the ways honesty is perceived, in beliefs about crime, and in ideas of justice. People from different groups have very different values regarding the matters that honesty tests measure. Accordingly, honesty tests should be permitted to incorporate these varied aspects of the constructs they measure. The law needs to be changed in this respect.

But even more important is the fact that there are major divisions in our society regarding key issues of justice and morality. For several years now we have been "crying in the wilderness" on this issue, based on our honesty test results. Now, with the O. J. Simpson verdict in Los Angeles, society is becoming more aware of existing disparities in guiding perceptions, beliefs, and values. John Leo, in a *U.S. News and World Report* editorial (1995), discusses this issue, and presents examples of how juries of different compositions view crime in different ways.

CONCLUSIONS

Much of the discussion related to discrimination charges deals with adverse impact. Test publishers emphasize that their products do not produce adverse impact, or at least adverse impact against protected groups. Studies comparing mean scores in different groups are widely utilized to make this point.

However, those who use honesty tests, or are considering doing so, need to keep two factors in mind. One is that adverse impact is not the overriding consideration; business necessity is. Good, solid evidence of validity, based on multiple studies of different types and carried out with different groups, may not always be politically palatable, but it is what matters ultimately in a court of law. The arguments presented by ideological proponents of equal employment opportunity often ignore the role of business necessity, because their goal is to achieve zero adverse impact, even at the cost of lowered business productivity. But that is not the way the law reads.

Second, ignoring the fact that an honesty test has adverse impact on non-protected groups, such as white males and younger workers, may not be very wise. To date reverse discrimination cases have not been frequent or widely successful, but they have been won and the concept is clearly established in law. It was the underlying factor behind the proscription of subgroup norming in the Civil Rights Act of 1991. However, anyone who has followed the field of employment discrimination over the years knows that things can change rapidly. A spate of reverse discrimination filings could change the law away from its original intent of protecting minorities and women. Thus, a close monitoring of legal developments on this score seems warranted.

The Civil Rights Act of 1991, with its prohibition on subgroup norming, introduces another consideration that honesty test users must take into account. It now becomes important to know exactly how a test was developed and whether the test publisher has made any adjustments to the scores. The law reinforces the need for test users to become involved in establishing cutting scores if they are necessary, and to know what is happening in that regard. The EEOC could endorse applying the subgroup norming ban to mental ability tests only, thus relieving honesty tests of this concern. It is important to monitor developments in this area. However, the delay has been sufficiently long so that we feel action of this kind by EEOC is unlikely. It will probably take action by Congress to correct the situation.

8

Honesty Testing and the Law: The Americans with Disabilities Act

Laws that deal with the disabled are concerned with employment discrimination, and in this sense fall within the purview of Chapter 7. However, in a number of respects this legislation is very different from the laws considered in the previous chapter. Treatment in a separate chapter is therefore required.

THE NATURE OF THE ACT

For many years, the major federal legislation dealing with discrimination against people with disabilities was the Rehabilitation Act of 1973, which applied only to the federal government, federal contractors, and recipients of federal financial assistance. With the passage of the Americans with Disabilities Act (ADA) in 1990, and its implementation for many employers in 1992, the scope of this type of legislation was expanded dramatically. The act is concerned with equal employment opportunities, requires equal availability and accessibility to all services provided by governments, and prohibits discrimination in public accommodations and services operated by a wide range of businesses serving the public.

In their article in *Personnel Journal* (1992) Wayne Barlow and Edward Hane summarize the legal obligations of the act for human resource management:

1. An employer must not deny a job to a disabled individual because of a disability if the individual is qualified and able to perform the essential functions of the job, with or without reasonable accommodation.

2. If an individual who has a disability is otherwise qualified but unable to perform an essential function without an accommodation, the employer must make a reasonable accommodation unless the accommodation would result in undue hardship.

3. An employer is not required to lower existing performance standards for a job when

considering the qualifications of an individual who has a disability if the standards are job-related and uniformly applied to all employees and candidates for that job.

4. Qualification standards and selection criteria that screen out or tend to screen out an individual on the basis of a disability must be job-related and consistent with business necessity.

5. Any test or other procedure used to evaluate qualifications must reflect the skills and abilities of an individual rather than impaired sensory, manual, or speaking skills, unless those are the job-related skills that the test is designed to measure. (p. 59)

Employers are required to make available an equal opportunity for those with disabilities to take part in the job application process and to be considered for a job. They may not inquire prior to actual employment with regard to a disability, but they may ask questions to determine whether a person has the ability to perform specific job activities. They may even ask for a demonstration of how these activities may be performed.

Employers cannot require that a medical examination be taken prior to an actual offer of employment. However, a job offer may be made conditional on the outcome of such an examination, conducted after the offer. Then all entering employees in a given job must take the examination. Tests for illegal drugs may be carried out pre-offer; they are not considered medical examinations under the law.

A disability is defined as follows:

1. A physical or mental impairment that substantially limits one or more of the major life activities of such individuals.

2. A record of such an impairment.

3. Being regarded as having such an impairment.

There are certain ambiguities in the act related to testing, and there are other concerns regarding the way a position is defined under the law. These and other considerations caused Freedley Hunsicker, a lawyer, to write at an early point in *Personnel Journal* (1990): "Although sweeping in scope, the ADA is hardly clear and comprehensive in its definition of essential terms. Consequently, confusion regarding its application is expected to be widespread."

Several years later, as ADA-related complaints continued to pile up in the federal enforcement agencies, Larry Reynolds, writing in *HR Focus* noted, "The far-reaching nature and vagueness of the legislation, however, have left most human resources departments unsure of what is required of them in specific situations" (1993, p. 6). A year later Reynolds wrote, "Just when employers thought they were getting a handle on the ADA, several new items have emerged on the regulatory agenda to further complicate the issue. ADA continues to provoke three key questions: What is a disability? Is it covered under ADA? Should it be covered under ADA?" (1994, p. 1).

There is no question that the ADA, like the Civil Rights Act of 1991, has engendered a great deal of uncertainty, in large part because of ambiguities and deficiencies in wording. Almost two years after the law went into effect, EEOC did issue enforcement guidance in an attempt to clarify some of these issues. These guidelines are much more specific than the legislation itself and should prove useful to employers. However, they do not have the force of law, and the courts still must decide whether the EEOC guidelines reflect the law's intent. A good supplemental source of information in this regard is the book by Jeffrey Allen entitled *Complying with the ADA* (1993).

Several articles provide a useful service by outlining what companies should do to comply with the ADA. Among these are an article by John Kohl and Paul Greenlaw in *Sloan Management Review* (1992) and another by Wayne Barlow in *Personnel Journal* (1991). These articles say:

1. Be aware that compliance with the ADA will involve hidden and, as yet, unknown indirect costs. Costly activities will include job analysis and job redesign.

2. Prepare by undertaking job analyses to determine the essential and marginal functions of jobs.

3. Train managers and supervisors involved in selection and other key employment decisions to identify and act appropriately with respect to individuals who have any disability.

4. Review job requirements to ensure that there is a direct relationship with the ability to perform essential functions of the job, consistent with business necessity. Employers should be prepared to identify the essential and non-essential functions of any job so that they may, in turn, evaluate and implement any available accommodation.

5. Be in a position to articulate legitimate, non-discriminatory, credible facts on which any employment decision is based. Such facts must include review of available accommodations considered, and the specific reason for employer rejection, all accommodations offered, and the individual's response to them.

6. Educate and coordinate with medical professionals who will be performing medical evaluations and examinations where permitted.

The impact of ADA on human resource activities covers a wide range. However, for honesty testing the most significant issues involve the making (or not making) of certain kinds of pre-employment inquiries and the conduct of medical examinations.

With regard to the latter, physical examinations may no longer be given early in the selection process. They are permissible only after a person has qualified for employment on other grounds and has been given a conditional hiring offer.

This offer of employment may be withdrawn, based on a physical examination administered after the job offer, under certain very specific conditions. As described by Michael Lotito and Jamerson Allen in the Society for Human Resource Management's *Legal Report* (1992) the appropriate legal reasons for withdrawing an offer are:

1. The examination revealed the individual could not perform the essential functions of the position with or without reasonable accommodation.
2. The individual would pose a significant risk of substantial harm—a "direct threat"—to the health or safety of others (and possibly the individual) which cannot be eliminated or reduced by reasonable accommodation.
3. The examination or related inquiry revealed that the individual lied on the employment application.
4. The individual tested positive for illegal drug use.
5. The individual previously submitted a fraudulent workers' compensation claim. (p. 6)

IS AN HONESTY TEST A MEDICAL EXAMINATION?

Shortly after the passage of the ADA, there was considerable concern as to whether honesty tests might be considered medical in nature. They clearly deal with personality traits, and personality is involved in mental disorders of various kinds which in turn are considered disabilities under the Act. Following this logic, honesty tests could only be administered subsequent to an initial job offer and thus after many job applicants had already been eliminated by other selection techniques. The resulting impact on the honesty test market, and on the market for personality tests in general, would be substantial. The uncertainties of this period are elaborated in articles by Dianne Brown in *The Industrial-Organizational Psychologist* (1992) and by David Arnold and Alan Thiemann in the *Journal of Business and Psychology* (1992).

It was not until mid-1994 with the issuance of the EEOC enforcement guidance that these anxieties over the status of testing began to be dispelled. The EEOC noted a number of considerations that should be taken into account in determining whether a test or procedure is a medical examination:

1. Whether the procedure or test is one that is administered by either a health care professional (including doctors, nurses, psychologists and other mental health professionals, physical and occupational therapy professionals, and others in the health care field) or someone trained by a health care professional.
2. Whether the results of the procedure or test are interpreted by either a health care professional or someone trained by a health care professional.
3. Whether the procedure or test is designed to reveal the existence, nature, or severity of an impairment, or the subject's general physical or psychological health.
4. Whether the employer is administering the procedure or test for the purpose of revealing the existence, nature, or severity of an impairment, or the subject's general physical or psychological health.
5. Whether the procedure or test is invasive and thus requires the drawing of blood, urine, breath, etc.
6. Whether the procedure or test measures physiological or psychological responses of an individual, as opposed to the individual's performance of a task.

7. Whether the procedure or test would normally be administered in a medical setting such as a health care professional's office or a hospital.

8. Whether medical equipment or devices are used in administering the procedure or test. (pp. 28–29)

It may take one or a number of these factors to make a determination. An example cited by the EEOC is that of a test designed to reveal mental illness, such as paranoia or depression, which is nevertheless used in the hiring process to disclose tastes and habits. The test is interpreted by a psychologist and is routinely used in clinical settings for diagnosing mental illness. Such a test would be considered a medical examination and could not be administered pre-offer.

Although these guidelines would seem to remove honesty testing from the medical examination category, problems could arise with personality-based tests having their origins in clinical practice. In making a decision with regard to the use of a particular test, it appears wise to become fully informed regarding its origins and the settings and purposes for which it was designed.

The EEOC does consider various kinds of testing procedures, and it offers guidance as to the stage of the hiring process when each may be applied. Thus:

Employers currently administer a wide variety of examinations which may be characterized as psychological in nature, including various types of I.Q. tests, aptitude tests, personality tests, and honesty tests. These examinations are intended to measure an individual's capacity and propensity to successfully perform a job. For example, applicants for nuclear power plant positions are sometimes given examinations designed to reflect whether they tend to be suitable for shift work, and/or whether they are likely to respond appropriately in the event of an emergency. Applicants for cash handling positions are sometimes given written examinations designed to reflect whether they are likely to steal money from the employer.

Psychological examinations would be considered medical examinations to the extent that they provide evidence concerning whether an applicant has a mental disorder or impairment, as categorized in the American Psychiatric Association's most recent *Diagnostic and Statistical Manual of Mental Disorders* [1994].

If a test was not designed to assess the existence, nature, or severity of an applicant's mental impairment, or an applicant's general psychological health, it still may be considered a medical examination if it is used by an employer to assess whether an applicant has a mental impairment or to assess an applicant's general psychological health.

On the other hand, to the extent that a test is designed and used to measure only such factors as an applicant's honesty, tastes, and habits, it would not normally be considered a medical examination.

An example of where a test can be considered medical in nature, and thus relegated to post-offer status, is an examination that measures excessive anxiety, depression, or certain compulsive disorders in applicants. A second example would be an examination designed to measure an applicant's aptitude for mechanical operations, which has been keyed with the help of a psychologist to establish patterns of answers on the test indicating that an applicant may have a psychological impairment. On the other hand, a personality test designed and used to indicate whether an applicant is likely to lie is not a medical examination, and accordingly may be given at the pre-offer stage.

EEOC also discusses tests of physical agility and fitness, polygraph examinations, vision tests, and drug or alcohol tests. Examples show when these procedures are and are not medical examinations. Insofar as honesty tests are concerned, these discussions add little to what has already been said. On balance it now appears that most honesty tests do not violate the ADA and can be administered early in the selection process. The only concern should be whether a test, or a special scoring key, has been tied at some point to one or more types of mental illness or impairment. It might be well to look at the various subscales of a multi-purpose honesty test, for instance, to be sure that none is labeled or used to identify a mental disorder.

DOES THE TEST CONTAIN PROHIBITED PRE-OFFER QUESTIONS?

The ADA prohibits making inquiries at the pre-offer stage that are likely to elicit information about a disability. If a question can reasonably be expected to elicit a response indicating that the individual has a disability, it should not be asked. Not only are direct questions regarding the presence of a disability proscribed, but inquiries that are so closely related to a disability that they are likely to reveal the disability are proscribed as well. Thus, questions regarding medications should be avoided because certain medications are typically prescribed for specific conditions.

Prohibitions of this kind are primarily relevant for interviewers and in constructing application forms. However, even if a psychological test is not in and of itself a medical examination, it may contain questions embedded in it that relate to the existence, nature, or severity of a disability, and which accordingly are prohibited at the pre-offer stage. This means that it is necessary for a test user to go through the test item-by-item and consider the legality of each question if the test is to be used pre-offer. Presumably the test publisher has done this, but if there is a slip-up the test user is not excused from responsibility.

The types of questions that must be avoided include the following:

1. Inquiries about whether an individual has sought or is currently seeking mental health services.

2. Inquiries about the extent of prior illegal drug use.

3. Most inquiries about prior or current lawful drug use.

4. Inquiries reflecting the extent of prior or current alcohol use, because these may reveal whether an individual is an alcoholic.

Questions related to drug and alcohol use and addiction are particularly difficult, but still important for honesty testing. In general, the ADA allows employers more latitude with regard to drugs than alcohol; pre-offer drug testing is permitted for instance, but similar alcohol testing is not. With respect to drug use it is permissible to ask, "Have you ever illegally used drugs?" and "Have you used cocaine in the last two years?" on the assumption that these questions do not necessarily deal with addiction. Asking about the extent or amount of drug use does relate to addiction, however, and is proscribed at the pre-offer stage. A good in-depth discussion of these issues is contained in an article by Jonathan Segal published in *HR Magazine* (1992).

WHAT ACCOMMODATIONS ARE REQUIRED IN ADMINISTERING TESTS?

Some people, because of their disabilities, cannot complete an honesty test in the regular, standardized manner. They need some kind of accommodation, a change in the way that the test is administered, to complete this aspect of the hiring process. EEOC makes it clear that reasonable accommodation of this kind should be provided if the applicant asks for it.

The process works as follows:

The employer states on the application form or job advertisement that all applicants must complete a written examination of some specified duration. Applicants are asked to inform the employer within a certain time (say 3 days) if, as a result of a disability, they will need an accommodation to take this test. Requests of this kind are not considered prohibited pre-offer inquiries and in fact, if the employer so indicates, must be supported by documentation from an appropriate professional. (EEOC 1994, pp. 15–17)

In contrast to the General Aptitude Test Battery (GATB) where, as Ramzi Baydoun and George Neumann point out in their *Journal of Business and Psychology* article (1992), many sections are timed to reward rapid responses and others require hand, finger, and eye coordination, honesty tests usually require less by way of accommodation. Nevertheless, there may be a need for accommodation, and ADA makes it necessary to deal with these needs in an acceptable manner.

As Mary Anne Nester notes in her paper entitled *Implementing the Americans with Disabilities Act: Pre-Employment Testing and the ADA* (1994), testing accommodations take three forms: testing format, time limits, and test content. Testing format changes include presentations in braille, using large print, having readers present items orally, and providing audiotapes. Time-limit changes typically permit more time on timed tests; people with learning disabilities might be given longer to respond, for instance. Test content changes include rewording items or even eliminating certain items. Long passages may need to be shortened for blind people for instance, simply because these passages place excessive demands on memory.

Honesty tests, like other written tests, may require format changes. Since most honesty tests are not timed, or if there is a time limit it plays a small role in the final score, time limit changes are unlikely to be a problem. Content changes probably would not be required, although some scenario items with a number of multiple-choice alternatives can be difficult to hold in mind if presented orally.

The problem with these accommodations is that they often change the nature of the test. It simply is not possible to make a meaningful comparison between the score of a disabled person taking a test one way and the scores of people without disabilities taking it another way. This factor is discussed by Richard Arvey and Paul Sackett in their chapter published in *Personnel Selection in Organizations* (1993). The more extensive the accommodations, the less comparability can be assured. On honesty tests, time changes usually do not matter a great deal and content changes are not likely to be required. Format changes are an issue, but the situation does not differ greatly from where people lack English language skills (see Chapter 6).

The greatest difficulty is that under the ADA everyone has to be evaluated in the same way—disabled or not. Thus, if honesty is at issue, honesty needs to be assessed for every applicant. Given this situation, and the fact that people who are not screened out have no basis for filing a discrimination complaint, we suspect that most disabled people for whom a reasonable accommodation (in the form of testing changes) is not really available will subsequently be judged acceptable on this part of the selection process irrespective of the truth.

CLOSE TO HOME: HOW AN HONESTY TEST DIED AS THE ADA WAS BORN

At numerous points throughout this book we have drawn on our own experience with an honesty test to illustrate various issues. The advent of the ADA provides another such opportunity. Remember that at the time the law went into effect there was a great deal of uncertainty regarding the meaning of many of its clauses and how the courts would interpret them.

Faced with this uncertainty and concerned about the possibilities of legal action under the ADA involving the test, a request was forwarded to the company's law firm for a review relative to ADA considerations. The legal opinion received is presented on the following pages.

The ADA specifically prohibits pre-employment inquiries about disabilities or which would be likely to lead to gaining information on disabilities. The EEOC's Compliance Manual breaks down the hiring process into two parts: Stage 1 (pre-employment) and Stage 2 (post-offer). The Compliance Manual discusses what should be included in each stage of the hiring process in detail. Prior to discussing the ADA's impact on the specific (honesty test) questions, I thought it helpful to set forth the interpretative guidance applicable here.

I. STAGE 1: PRE-OFFER

Before making a conditional offer, an employer may not make any medical inquiries or ask any questions which might reveal medical information. The Compliance Manual expressly notes that at this stage an employer:
—*may* ask questions about an applicant's ability to perform specific job functions;
—*may not* make an inquiry about a disability;
—*may* make a job offer that is conditioned on satisfactory results of a *post-offer* medical examination or inquiry.

II. STAGE 2: POST-OFFER

After making a conditional job offer and before an individual starts work, an employer may conduct a medical examination or ask health-related questions, providing that all candidates who receive a conditional job offer in the same job category are required to take the same examination or respond to the same inquiries. It is also *recommended* that background checks, drug tests and workers' compensation inquiries, as well as medical examinations, be reserved for this stage.

Post-Offer Items:

- **Background Checks**

Although pre-offer background checks are not *per se* illegal under ADA, it is advisable to reserve such checks until after making a conditional offer. A routine reference check may reveal a disability, as could interviews involved in a background check, and the employer risks an inference being drawn from such pre-employment knowledge.

- **Drug Testing**

Drug tests are expressly excluded from the ADA's definition of medical examinations which cannot be conducted prior to a job offer. However, in order to be meaningful, a drug test must include questions about prescription drugs. The EEOC Compliance Manual specifically states that such inquiries are prohibited, and suggests that drug tests be conducted post-offer for this reason.

- **Workers' Compensation**

No questions about previous workers' compensation claims should be asked before an offer of employment is made. Questions which would assist an employer in making a second injury fund claim are specifically permitted post-offer.

- **Medical Examinations**

An employer may condition a job offer on the satisfactory result of a post-offer medical examination or medical inquiry if this is required of all entering employees in the same category. This medical examination or inquiry is not limited in scope and need not be job-related and consistent with business necessity. However, if the inquiry results in screening out an individual because of a disability, the *exclusion* must be job-related and consistent with business necessity. In addition, it is important to note that medical examinations of *employees* must be job-related and consistent with business necessity, except that an employer may maintain a *voluntary* medical examination program.

With regard to psychological and similar tests, some tests will certainly be considered medical examinations, and thus prohibited until the post-offer stage, while others may be arguably considered not to be medical examinations. The tests which may not be medical examinations would be personality tests which are designed to determine whether an individual's personality is well-suited for a specific job. An example of this would be a personality test given to potential sales employees. However, psychological examinations which are designed to determine whether a person is mentally fit to hold a specific position would be clearly medical examinations. For example, a psychological test given to a nuclear employee to ensure psychological or mental stability, a measure of reliability and trustworthiness would clearly be a medical examination.

While the [honesty test] does not appear to fall unequivocally under either of these two categories, I believe its designed intent to measure honesty or integrity tendencies can be described as constructs to assess psychological or mental stability. As a result, it is recommended the test be administered, if at all, at the post-offer stage.

Would the Company be subject to liability if it were to extend an offer and then withdraw it based upon the outcome of the [honesty test]? Of course, it is very important that when the offer is extended, it is made clear that the offer is conditional upon the individual's ability to perform the essential functions of the position being offered, as well as the individual's background check and other tests, including the [honesty test], having a satisfactory outcome. In that way, the Company will not be subject to any contractual liability upon withdrawing an offer.

Of course, concerns about the liability of withdrawing an offer go beyond contractual concerns, and to the heart of the Americans with Disabilities Act. Obviously, any time that you withdraw an offer at the post-offer stage, you should be prepared to defend your decision against challenge in an agency or court setting. An individual with a disability may well file a charge of discrimination or lawsuit because of the withdrawal of the conditional offer.

The [honesty test] should in no case be given before the post-offer stage because the test appears to be a prohibited medical examination.

The preceding is what the law firm had to say about the medical examination issue, and the stage at which the honesty test should be administered. Understand that moving honesty testing to a post-offer stage substantially constricts the market for a test. Whereas at pre-offer any applicant for a position can be and probably would be tested, at post-offer only those select few who are deemed fully employable, based on the information then available, take the test. This downward shift in the available market normally would be expected to drive the price per test up as sales quantities are reduced. However, what if the competition does not view the legal context in the same way? What if they interpret the ADA as permitting pre-offer testing? Then prices could not be raised and the company would be at a severe competitive disadvantage. This is the source of the dilemma our firm and others like it faced as the ADA came on stream.

A second issue that the law firm addressed was the wording of specific questions within the test. Here the legal review reached the following conclusions:

Even if the [honesty test] is reserved for the post-offer stage, it does raise some concerns about potential adverse impact upon individuals with disabilities. Unlike Title VII, the ADA specifically prohibits certain pre-employment inquiries. However, this law firm has long advised clients not to ask questions in interviews or on application forms, unless the responses to them can be legally considered in making an employment decision. For example, an employer should not ask an individual his age, except to ask if he is over 18 in order to help the employer comply with child labor laws. Moreover, an employer should not ask an employee if he is a U.S. citizen, because the employer is not permitted to discriminate on the basis of immigrant status.

When an employer asks a question of an applicant concerning information which cannot be considered in making an employment decision, courts have long held that such a question may constitute evidence of discriminatory intent if the applicant is not hired. Similarly, it is possible that case law may develop under the Americans with Disabilities Act concerning inquiries made at the post-offer stage, which are not specifically prohibited by the Americans with Disabilities Act, but which may not legally be used in making employment decisions.

With these considerations in mind, the following is a list of questions in the [honesty test] which may raise concerns under the ADA, even if they are asked at the post-offer stage.

The [honesty test] should be given only at the post-offer stage, and only if the questions creating concerns here have been modified to comply with the Americans with Disabilities Act.

Of the 82 scorable questions in the honesty test, 21 (over 25 percent) were then said to raise concerns of some kind. Most frequently the concern was expressed as follows—It is recommended not to have a question of this kind in this test to avoid any possibility that the results are infected by a disparate impact upon individuals with such a disability. The disability most frequently causing the concern was drug addiction.

Given the already reduced number of scorable items produced by moving to a single, all-purpose scoring key to comply with the Civil Rights Act of 1991, this further reduction presented major difficulties. We were coming close to a test with too few items to justify its existence on reliability grounds. Obviously to continue testing we needed to develop new items, compare them with polygraph results, and then validate the new items selected following the previous test development strategy. Unfortunately, however, the Employee Polygraph Protection Act of 1988 had now intervened, and following that strategy would be much more difficult.

The ring of the law firm's final conclusion had the sound of a death knell:

The [honesty test] should in no case be given before the post-offer stage because the test appears to be a prohibited medical examination. In addition, certain questions on the test, even if it is given at the post-offer stage, may consitute evidence of discriminatory intent. Finally, some questions in the test as it is written now could result in the Company making decisions about employees based on a test which adversely impacts individuals with disabilities, and which seeks information indirectly which could not be sought directly. In that situation, the test could be found illegal, even though it is being given at the post-offer stage. Therefore, the [honesty test] should be given only at the post-offer stage, and only if the questions creating concerns here have been modified to comply with the Americans with Disabilities Act.

In fact, the entrepreneur who owned the business and had funded the test's development and marketing decided to cease operations at this point. The costs of continuing appeared excessive, the market appeared to have been substantially reduced, and there were major legal liabilities on the horizon that had not existed previously. It is ironic that this individual himself suffered from a disability which the ADA was intended to protect. In effect the Act ''shot down'' one of its own people. He took a loss of over $1 million.

We wish to emphasize that what happened was in large part a result of the uncertainty surrounding the ADA as it went into effect. There was an inordinate amount of room for varied interpretations. The article by Arnold and Thiemann noted earlier in this chapter which was published in the summer of 1992 reflects a completely different legal interpretation from the one we have just described. They say:

[C]ommonly used psychological tests are not medical in nature, nor are they utilized to identify disabilities when used for employment screening. Thus, the specific time when such tests may be administered is not controlled by the ADA.

and again:

[T]here is a broad set of traits which employers may legally inquire about at the pre-employment stage. The only limitation on the use of any preemployment psychological test is that the test may not disclose a mental or psychological disorder.

and still later:

While there are tests whose purpose and use is to detect a mental impairment, they represent a small minority of the tests which are used in employment settings. The vast majority of tests used in employment settings are used to assess applicants with respect to qualities which are not even remotely similar to those contained in the definition of impairment.

These legal interpretations served to influence one of our major competitors in the honesty testing arena. Thus, if we had continued operations we would have been competing in the small, post-offer market, while leaving the much larger, pre-offer market entirely to the competition.

As the clouds have cleared and the meaning of the ADA has become more apparent, we now believe the Arnold and Thiemann view is the correct one for most honesty testing. It is a view consistent with the enforcement guidance from the EEOC published in May 1994 and the conclusions we have noted in prior sections of this chapter. Nevertheless, our example shows the effects that unclearly worded laws may have, and it highlights the kinds of dilemmas companies may face in dealing with the legislation of the future.

CONCLUSIONS

The key consideration under the Americans with Disabilities Act now appears to be that employers cannot initially do anything to establish whether an applicant does or does not have a disability. You are simply not supposed to know, and any avenue that might provide this information is closed off until a conditional offer has been made. Then you have to show that if an offer is withdrawn it is because you have found out about a disability which would, in fact, interfere with effective performance of crucial job functions. The Act is very thorough in keeping those who might intend to discriminate against the disabled from having the information that would permit them to do so. It tends to assume discriminatory intent unless there is good reason to assume otherwise.

For honesty testing the most likely impairments that might be revealed, and should not be, are various mental disorders, including drug addiction and alcohol addiction. Criminal activities per se present no problems under the ADA, unless their existence would indirectly reveal the presence of a disability.

Certain states have laws related to disabilities and inquiries regarding disabilities that are even more stringent than the ADA. In these cases the state laws take precedence. Otherwise the federal ADA is the law of the land.

9

Privacy Considerations: Legal and Otherwise

There is no overarching federal law on privacy rights, although laws of this kind have been considered by Congress on occasion. The U.S. Constitution does not explicitly guarantee privacy, but the Supreme Court, nevertheless, has mentioned or recognized such a right in various decisions, drawing upon various amendments to the Constitution. A number of federal laws deal with privacy considerations in one context or another. In general, these laws protect the privacy of government employees more than employees in the private sector, although the Employee Polygraph Protection Act of 1988 does the reverse.

Some state constitutions provide for privacy protections. A number of states have passed privacy laws of one kind or another, although employment matters in the private sector are covered less often than other types of privacy. Also, states may recognize a common law cause of action for invasion of privacy. In general, the state protections are a patchwork. Honesty tests may run afoul of them, but to date few such cases have been brought. This may be because there is no relevant law in a given jurisdiction, or because few people are aware of laws that do exist.

PRIVACY VALUES

Certainly privacy is a strongly held value in the United States, quite independent of whether that value is codified in law. Honesty tests can violate that value because they inquire about things that people believe they should have the right to keep to themselves. This is a particular concern if the test is administered to current employees, and test completion is a condition for continued employment. On the other hand, answering the questions is more a voluntary matter when honesty tests are used for pre-employment screening. Applicants can protect their privacy without suffering any severe damage by simply declining to complete the test, and if that is not acceptable applying for work elsewhere.

Privacy values may influence both employers and applicants. Some organizations do not use honesty tests because of concerns about the impact that the testing would have on the image of the organization. In many such cases, strong employer values are involved. It simply feels wrong to ask job applicants questions that you yourself would not want to answer. There are companies that will not let a salesperson for an honesty test in the door. The company has a policy against using such a test, and so there is no point in discussing the matter.

When a firm has a serious honesty problem, we find this type of policy difficult to justify. Furthermore, using overt honesty tests can create a climate for honesty that extends well beyond the mere screening out of problem employees. Nevertheless, privacy values do influence employers and the policies they establish.

We provided a review of the research dealing with applicant reactions to honesty tests in Chapter 5, under the heading Applicant Reactions and Impressions. Where honesty considerations are obviously important in a job, applicants on the average do not appear to be greatly concerned about the violation of privacy values. Honesty tests tend to be viewed as being at about the midpoint when selection procedures are ranked in terms of how invasive they are. Eugene and Diana Stone report a study in *Research in Personnel and Human Resource Management* (1990) in which the ranking was as follows:

1 Lie detector		Most Invasive
2 Drug test		
3 Medical examination to assess disease potential		
4 Background check		
5 Medical examination to assess actual disease		
6 *Honesty test*		
7 Personality inventory		
8 Mental ability test		
9 Physical ability test		
10 Work sample		
11 Interview		
12 Application blank		Least Invasive

Honesty tests appear to be viewed much like other personality tests in this regard. Such tests have been attacked for their violation of privacy values, dating back at least to William Whyte's bestseller *The Organization Man*, first published in 1956. Some people clearly feel strongly about their privacy, and indict personality tests, and in more recent years honesty tests, as a consequence. Most people, although they are not overjoyed at the prospect of taking the tests, have come to accept them as a necessary part of obtaining certain kinds of jobs. Some may even find them intriguing.

Our research suggests that roughly 5 percent of all applicants have serious concerns about the kinds of questions asked, although not necessarily to the point of refusing to answer them. Privacy values are a factor that those who use honesty tests must consider. Yet they are not a major public concern.

However, those who do believe the tests violate their strong values are the most likely to bring legal actions, if they are in a jurisdiction where this is possible. We need to give special attention to this matter.

THE LEGAL CONTEXT

Anne Libbin, Susan Mendelsohn, and Dennis Duffy, writing in *Personnel* (1988), have this to say about the legal context of honesty testing:

[H]onesty tests may create as many legal problems as they are designed to solve. Many critics argue that because they frequently probe into the employee's attitudes toward religion and sex, and examine his or her family relationships, personal habits, and private interests, honesty tests violate the employee's right to privacy, and psychological tests which have been designed for a purpose other than job screening are especially suspect. However, the courts have been willing to allow employers to use such tests when the employer can show that they are job related. (p. 47)

The job-relatedness requirement should immediately trigger thoughts of job descriptions and job analysis whenever it is mentioned, as here. If the job is one where honesty considerations are shown to be important, then honesty tests seem more relevant to the courts.

Also, in dealing with privacy violations the courts have generally sought to balance the interests of the individual against those of both the employing organization and the public. The courts have argued that in instances where there is a compelling public interest, the privacy rights of an individual should be subordinated to that interest. Many of these cases have involved drug testing, where public safety is at risk, but the same type of argument would seem applicable to honesty testing.

Generally, where legal actions are initiated involving honesty tests, it is the content of specific test items that is at issue, not the test as a whole. The book by Michael O'Bannon, Linda Goldinger, and Gavin Appleby entitled *Honesty and Integrity Testing* (1989) contains a good discussion of privacy considerations and the law. That discussion ends with the following comment:

Because most states have not extensively utilized privacy torts in the context of employee selection devices, this is not currently a major consideration in the honesty testing decision. The use of some questions in these tests, however, may make for a close call on this issue. Questions pertaining to past commission of a crime, whether theft-related or not, may lead to allegations of invasion of privacy. Where a state has created relatively strong protections of privacy for its citizens, an employer may want to consider using a less intrusive test. At a minimum, the employer requesting this type of information should not utilize test answers in a criminal context such as providing them to the police.

Rather, an employer should inform test-takers that test results will be kept confidential. In fact, the safest course of action is to keep confidential all test results, including honesty test information, to minimize the likelihood of privacy concerns. (p. 108)

We would strongly endorse the call for maintaining the confidentiality of answers to test questions and of test scores. Issues related to the legality of asking specific questions must be answered on a jurisdiction-by-jurisdiction basis.

It is important to recognize, however, that it is not only privacy law that bears on the legality of specific questions. Much more frequently questions are proscribed by state laws dealing with discrimination in employment. Because the body of law is more fully developed in this area, those who feel their privacy rights have been violated by the questions contained in a test may well bring suit under other legislation dealing with equal employment opportunities.

An article by Philip Ash in the *Journal of Business and Psychology* (1991b) describes the various types of questions that it is unwise to ask in various states. The issues that are regulated by the states are often published in lists of impermissible questions; they apply to such matters as age, arrests, convictions, economic status, education, and so on. In most cases the intent is to remove these questions from interviews and application forms, but the strictures typically apply as well to any type of test used in selection.

Ash provides information on 16 types of questions. The states most active in this regard are Colorado (14 areas); Arizona, Illinois, New Jersey, and West Virginia (13 areas), California, Missouri, Ohio, and Washington (12 areas); and Hawaii, Nevada, New York, and Rhode Island (11 areas). Questions directly or indirectly dealing with applicant sex are the most frequently proscribed (31 states). Next most frequent are questions related to nationality (28 states), followed by those involving age and race (both 24 states), mental or physical health (23 states), height and weight including photographs (22 states), and religion (21 states). The close tie between these proscriptions and federal anti-discrimination law is clearly evident.

With regard to these state laws, Ash says the following:

Although the regulations are numerous, and frequently confusingly diverse, and the issues involved are sometimes critically important to employment applicants, the body of case law and discursive analysis that exists is surprisingly small. It may well be the case that states with extensive regulations respecting preemployment inquiries simply do not have the capability to monitor the area very much, and that applicants may, on the one hand, be unaware of proscriptions on particular inquiries, and, on the other, reluctant or unable to do much about them. (p. 305)

Another avenue for enforcing privacy rights is polygraph legislation. At the federal level, this appears unlikely insofar as honesty tests are concerned, since a clause specifically prohibiting these tests was withdrawn from the polygraph bill prior to its passage. Some state laws, however, are written more broadly and might be used to block honesty testing. To date there is little evidence of this happening. A discussion of the issues involved is contained in the *Behavioral Sciences and the Law* article by Stephen Guastello and Mark Rieke (1991).

Irrespective of the avenue a challenge to honesty test questions might take, it appears that few such cases have been filed and even fewer won. Yet it is well to recognize that honesty tests are a type of personality test. The questions in these personality tests have long been under fire, and there is some evidence that the attack has shifted to the legal context in recent years. Consequently, Ash notes that, "Questions included in personality and attitude inventories could well be the next battlefield in the preemployment inquiry arena" (p. 305). The risk that honesty tests might be caught in the personality test net is always there.

STATE LEGISLATION FOCUSED ON HONESTY TESTING

To complete the picture of the legal context for honesty testing, we need to add legislation and legislative proposals that focus directly on the tests themselves in an effort to promote privacy rights. The most restrictive legislation of this type was passed in Massachusetts several years ago. John Jones, Philip Ash, Catalina Soto, and William Terris discuss this law in the book edited by Jones entitled *Preemployment Honesty Testing* (1991a). They indicate that companies in Massachusetts interested in reducing employee theft must substitute tests that measure "dependability" for overt honesty tests. Written honesty tests are barred completely, although the exact scope of the law remains unclear to this date.

Other states have considered a variety of bills which would outlaw or restrict honesty testing, with the avowed purpose of fostering privacy rights. David Arnold, in the *Journal of Business and Psychology* (1991), describes the situation in Oregon in considerable detail. He also provides information on a New York bill. Arnold has a note in *The Industrial-Organizational Psychologist* (1991) that focuses on the Oregon experience as well. A second article in this latter source written with Rachel Ankeny (1992) describes several other legislative initiatives, including the one in Rhode Island. Other states that have considered bills are Connecticut, South Dakota, and Virginia. In the typical scenario, one will find the American Psychological Association and the Association of Personnel Test Publishers opposing the legislation and the American Civil Liberties Union and perhaps organized labor supporting it.

To date, only the Massachusetts legislation has had a major impact on honesty testing. Rhode Island has a law that permits honesty testing, but only as long as the tests are not used to form the primary basis of an employment decision. Numerous other initiatives in Rhode Island, like those in the other states, have failed to achieve passage.

Historically, the pattern has been that social legislation is first passed in the states of the Northeast, particularly Massachusetts and New York. Then there is a gradual spread to other states, and finally federal legislation is established to create a "level playing field." Whether this pattern will be repeated in the case of honesty testing is an open question. American business now faces much greater competition from around the globe, often from countries that have very little restrictive legislation, than it did in the past. The U.S. Congress cannot act to create a truly level playing field in such a global economy. Whether this will serve to reverse the patterns developed earlier in this century is anybody's guess.

Certainly the move to limit honesty testing at the federal level is stalled for the moment, but given the fact that so few states have as yet established laws in this area of any kind, a federal law seems premature in any event. State activity in the name of privacy protection continues, however. David Arnold believes the initiatives he describes are unlikely to be isolated incidents. We suspect he is right.

CONCLUSIONS

Privacy values play an important role in American society and have done so throughout our country's history. Yet most people do not view honesty tests, appropriately administered, as representing an invasion of privacy to any substantial degree. There are, of course, exceptions. When these exceptions are employers, the company is likely to have a policy that bars the use of honesty tests. When the exception is an employee or job applicant, some kind of legal action may occur.

Privacy law is a complex patchwork at both the federal and state levels. In addition, laws created to deal with equal employment opportunity may be called upon to bring privacy actions as well. State anti-polygraph laws might be invoked, and some laws directly focused on honesty tests do exist.

If a company uses honesty tests on a widespread basis and over a considerable period of time, the possibility of legal action cannot be denied. Based on past experience the risk is not high, but it is present. How, then, should a company deal with this risk?

Daniel O'Meara, a management attorney, provides suggestions in an *HR Magazine* article (1994).

1. Deal with an established, reputable organization.
2. Ask the test creator if the test has ever caused employment discrimination charges, or ever been scrutinized in any investigation. Ask if there has ever been an invasion of privacy lawsuit or any other litigation involving the test.

3. Ask if the test has ever been "validated" by the EEOC and, if so, the position(s) to which that validation applies. Ask for an opinion letter concerning the test's lawfulness under employment discrimination laws. Ask for an opinion letter that all the inquiries on the test are permissible in your state.

4. Ask for information on precise traits the test seeks to measure and objective proof that the test actually measures these traits. If the offer of proof of validity is difficult for you to understand, it will probably be difficult for an agency, judge or jury to understand.

5. Ask for an indemnification for attorney's fees and liability based on proper use of the test that results in litigation or agency investigation. Ensure that if litigation arises that the test creator will provide defense testimony at no charge.

6. Don't be satisfied with oral representations of a sales person. Ask for the assurances in writing. Discuss the proposed testing with your legal counsel. Consider asking your legal counsel to run a computer search for cases mentioning the test you are considering. (pp. 99–100)

We agree that companies should ask questions of this nature, if only to be prepared. In some instances, such as validation research, the lack of an appropriate answer should be a bar to using a particular test. In other instances that may not be the case; it depends on the specific nature of the answer. For instance, the EEOC does not validate tests, but under certain circumstances it does set forth opinions regarding them. The following paragraph from a response to an inquiry explains the EEOC's position:

The EEOC does not issue an approval/disapproval for "test" as a general operating procedure. If a "test" is alleged to be discriminatory in an employment related action by a charging party (adverse impact on a particular group of persons because of their race, sex, age, etc.), the EEOC, during the investigation of the charge, will review the test, the results of the test, any validation studies conducted and the application of the test in relation to its impact on the particular group in question. After such review, the Commission decides only if the test has a discriminatory impact on the protected class of individuals.

On occasion after an investigation, the EEOC will indicate that a test does not have a discriminatory impact, and that is helpful information. But the lack of any decision from the EEOC may only mean that no charges have been brought.

All in all it is best to use a test that appears most attractive in relation to O'Meara's questions. However, it must be recognized that larger test publishers, who sell many tests to many clients, are likely to experience more legal activity simply because of their greater exposure. Also, one can become so concerned with the possibility of litigation that other important considerations are ignored. Clearly the best way to avoid a lawsuit over honesty testing is not to test, but that does not help in solving the problems of a dishonest workforce.

10

Selling Honesty Tests

The American Psychological Association (APA) task force report on honesty testing contains the following statement:

Promotional claims for honesty tests, as perhaps for most other procedures used for pre-employment screening, vary from the circumspect to the fraudulent. We have seen a number of promotional brochures that are so clearly excessive and overblown as to make a test expert cringe in embarrassment. In the most flagrantly hucksterish of these, all problems associated with test use are unmentioned, and the purported reduction in actual theft that can be achieved is wildly exaggerated. We recommend that test publishers adopt and enforce standards ensuring that the promotional claims made by each testing organization rest on a firm empirical foundation. This includes expending company resources to train sales representatives about the statements and claims that are appropriate for each test, and to monitor the performance of these personnel. (pp. 20–21)

The book *Honesty in the Workplace* by Kevin Murphy (1993) has this to say:

The marketing of integrity tests is, in many cases, a disgrace. The APA report notes that the claims made for some of these tests are so excessive and overblown as to be fraudulent. Indeed, if you want to see examples of dishonesty in the workplace, you need not look much further than the marketing brochures for some integrity tests. Experts in consumer fraud warn us that claims that look too good to be true often *are* too good to be true. A marketing brochure that claims that a simple test will eliminate most or all of an organization's theft and shrinkage problems should not be taken seriously.

At least two groups suffer from the failure of some test publishers to live up to the standards that govern other types of testing: test consumers and the many integrity test publishers who do live up to these standards. Both organizations and individuals suffer when tests with limited validity or relevance are used to make important decisions. The entire integrity testing industry suffers because of the actions of those publishers who fail to conform to appropriate technical and ethical guidelines. (p. 129)

Paul Sackett, Laura Burris, and Christine Callahan in their *Personnel Psychology* review (1989) note that "As integrity tests are marketed in large part to nonpsychologists, these tests are marketed more aggressively than most psychological tests. Unfortunately, it is not uncommon to encounter questionable, if not blatantly deceptive, sales tactics" (p. 523). A similar conclusion is reached by Walter Haney, George Madaus, and Robert Lyons in their book *The Fractured Marketplace for Standardized Testing* (1993).

Obviously there is something here that needs to be discussed.

HOW HONESTY TESTS ARE SOLD

In most cases, and certainly among the larger publishers, honesty tests are sold via a two-step process. On the front line are salespeople who write to, call, and visit potential and existing clients. Usually these are individuals whose early sales experience was in some other industry. They typically have not had much formal training in test development and psychology, although many have learned from experience in the field and are able to talk the language of psychological testing rather well. The range of real knowledge is substantial. Some do not speak the language correctly. There is a tendency among professional psychologists to view this misspeak as deception and perhaps even deliberate fraud. It can be that, but we believe that more frequently than not it simply reflects the misunderstandings of less technically educated people operating in a highly sophisticated professional arena.

On the second line, in a backup role, are one or more professionally trained psychologists with Ph.D. degrees who enter the sales process to consolidate gains made by the salespeople. They make presentations to client groups, write letters to clients, prepare articles for publication, and the like. It is not uncommon for the salespeople to attribute considerable mystique to these individuals; these psychologists are the wizards who exercise an almost magical influence and who through their wisdom create the tests that uncover dishonesty. Some psychologists like this role and play it to the hilt, while others find it difficult. Irrespective of a psychologist's feelings, however, the way in which the sales process is structured and the nature of the product serve to foster this mystical role in any event.

These second-line psychologists typically are well-trained in the field. They know about their tests and what the tests can do. They know about research strategies and validation. Often they know a surprising amount about legalities as well; some, indeed, are lawyers as well as psychologists. Often they are spread very thin, in that they are doing many things at once. They may only be consultants to the test publishing firm, or they may be full-time employees. Either way their time is likely to be expensive. It may be difficult to get through to them unless it becomes absolutely necessary to consummate a sale or solve a problem. Yet from a company viewpoint getting through can be absolutely necessary. This is where the answers are. This is where the special needs of a particular test user can be served.

It is not our intent to denigrate the salespeople here. The point is that the first line is staffed with sales experts who can bring in customers. If sales can be made at this point, they cost less and the profit is higher. On the second line are the content experts who can nail down more difficult sales. The sales costs are greater when these people become involved, and the profit is less, but at least a sale which would otherwise be lost has a chance.

Essentially the same two-step process is applied in all cases. Some sales people find it easier to establish initial contacts with a human resource manager, or security, or line management, or even with a financial manager. Wherever they start, if they are good at their work, they find their way to the point within the company where a decision is made on honesty testing and on what test will be used. When they get to that point, they try to make the sale alone. Then they go to their backup, depending on what the client requires, the availability of a psychologist, cost considerations, and the like.

One common approach used to bring a backup psychologist into the sales process deserves particular attention. Let us assume that two test publishers are vying for a sales opportunity. The salesperson for one such company may at a certain point offer to obtain a letter from the psychological staff back at headquarters giving a professional assessment of the competing test. This letter invariably criticizes the competition and portrays the company's test in glowing terms.

It is important to recognize that the letter is part of the sales process and not the balanced, objective professional opinion that it may purport to be. The criticisms of the competition may or may not be correct. We believe that the best way to deal with situations of this kind is to share the letter with the competing company, and hear both sides of the story. This way the potential customer gets the maximum amount of information and any misrepresentations can be corrected.

VALUE CONTEXTS, COMPETITION, AND ETHICS

Selling honesty tests is a very competitive business; some would consider it too competitive. We do not think this is because the tests are sold to non-psychologists, as Paul Sackett and his co-authors suggest. Rather we believe that it is closely related to the controversy and strong values surrounding honesty testing that we discussed in Chapter 4.

The industry operates in a context of high emotion where people attack it in legislative halls, in publications, and from the speaker's rostrum. Many are trying to get laws passed that would eliminate the industry completely. Emotions run high and on occasion rationality gets lost. In this type of business climate, those who are out selling the tests tend to feel they are constantly under attack. Eventually they start attacking back. Sometimes they attack when there is nobody there.

This situation creates a kind of anything-goes orientation in the industry. It is an unfair world and if you do not take care of yourself no one else will. Ethics may well get lost in this type of context. We are not saying that the honesty testing industry is unique in this respect. We are saying that this is the way things are. And we have been there. Test users should be prepared for this hypercompetition.

COMPETITIVE MARKETING STRATEGIES

Given this situation, what competitive strategies are available? We address this issue with some trepidation because strategies often are not revealed by the firms that use them. We cannot discuss what is not apparent to us. Yet there are some approaches that are sufficiently obvious that we believe we can identify them.

One strategy is focused on price. The test publisher tries to underprice the competition, and to keep costs to a minimum. Quantity discounts are typical. These companies try very hard to make a sale at the point of contact without involving a backup psychologist. They also tend to minimize the training of their sales personnel. They simply cut costs to the bone, and pass the savings on to the customer, in an effort to underprice the competition and make a sale.

The result is that there typically is little research of any kind, and validation studies are infrequent. If the test-publisher is a psychologist there may be some up-front validation, but after that he/she becomes involved in selling, and has little time for additional studies.

From the viewpoint of a test user, this approach has the advantage that tests can be bought and scored at a low price. The problem is that it is difficult to know what you are getting, and you have little basis for defending it in court. In our opinion, this is a feasible option for test users only if they are prepared to do their own validation. Usually these publishers will commit to doing validation studies with you, as long as they do not have to bear the major research costs. What this requires is that you either have the research capability within your own organization, or you must hire a consultant to do the research for you.

In many cases the price advantage that a publisher offers, when a company will be using a large number of tests, is sufficient to justify this approach. You need to study the test closely to see if it contains questions that will pass the necessary legal scrutiny, and also questions that are likely to yield validity. After that, it is not very difficult to conduct your own studies using one or more of the validity study designs discussed in Chapter 3. It may actually cost less overall to hire your own consultant to do this research than to resort to a high-cost publisher that does it for you. It depends on your anticipated test volume.

This low-price strategy might be labeled the "low road." In contrast there is a "high road" which utilizes a more costly test, but with the assurance that all professional requirements have been met. When this strategy is followed fully, there are numerous validity studies available, many of them reported in the professional literature. The publisher offers to take over all aspects of the testing program. The user does not have to worry about anything.

This strategy creates an image of high integrity. Psychologists in these companies are often professionally active. They write, they speak at professional society meetings, they engage in a wide range of professional activities, and they tend to criticize ethical lapses by other firms. There has been a distinct tendency to disassociate themselves from the polygraph, especially since the passage of the Polygraph Protection Act.

From the perspective of the test user, firms that follow this strategy have a lot to offer. They invest in test development and validation. They tend to have available tests that are differentiated for various uses; there are numerous subscales. They keep on top of legal developments, and often are active in counteracting legislative initiatives that would restrict the industry. You pay for all this, but it may well be worth it. At various points we have argued that test users should not turn everything over to a publisher, however. Establishing cutting scores, doing training, looking into adverse impact—these are some of the issues that test users need to remain involved in. If you do utilize a firm that operates from a high-road strategy, it is important not to become so secure in the relationship that you are no longer fully aware of what is happening.

What we have described are two strategic extremes. Many firms fall at some point in-between. There are even some companies that do not follow any consistent strategy at all, tending to shift positions depending on circumstances and the particular influences to which strategic decision makers become exposed. Nevertheless, we believe the low-road versus high-road differentiation is a useful way of looking at competitive strategies in the honesty testing industry.

INDUSTRY SELF-POLICING

At several points in this book we have made reference to a document entitled *Model Guidelines for Preemployment Integrity Testing Programs*. This is a 20-page statement intended to establish standards for the honesty testing industry. It is in the tradition of the high-road strategy. It is important because it contains considerable information that should be useful to test users as they consider the sales appeals of various test publishers.

The *Model Guidelines* are the product of an industry group called the Association of Personnel Test Publishers, which has as its major goals the following:

1. To promote activities designed to ensure the highest level of professionalism among personnel test publishers and their clients.
2. To establish and maintain industry standards.

3. To cooperate and consult with all professional, legal, and business organizations that have an interest in the effectiveness of personnel testing practices.

4. To facilitate the sharing of information among personnel test publishers and other organizations, associations, and individuals involved in personnel testing for the purposes of establishing and maintaining professional standards.

5. To continually seek to improve both the public understanding and practice of psychological testing in general and personnel testing in particular.

The task force that prepared the guidelines consisted of 17 psychologists, most of whom have had extensive experience in the honesty testing industry. They were advised by another five psychologists who served as special contributors and representatives of four trade associations whose members are some of the major users of honesty tests.

The following is an overview of the contents of the guidelines.

I. INTRODUCTION

    A. The Association of Personnel Test Publishers: An Overview

    B. Task Force Members and Organizations Who Contributed to These Model Guidelines

    C. Background of Project

    D. Purpose of Model Guidelines

    E. Complementary Guidelines

    F. Non-proprietary versus Proprietary Tests

    G. Types of Integrity Tests

II. TECHNICAL AND ETHICAL GUIDELINES

    A. Model Guidelines for Test Publishers
        1. Test Development and Selection
        2. Test Administration and Scoring
        3. Test Use and Interpretation
        4. Test Fairness and Confidentiality
        5. Public Statements and Test Marketing

    B. Model Guidelines for Test Users
        1. Test Development and Selection
        2. Test Administration and Scoring
        3. Test Use and Interpretation
        4. Test Fairness and Confidentiality
        5. Public Statements and Test Marketing

III. REFERENCES

IV. APPENDIX: GLOSSARY OF KEY TERMS

An article by John Jones, David Arnold, and William Harris in the *Journal of Business and Psychology* (1990) provides more information. It is apparent that the *Model Guidelines* were strongly influenced by several of the larger companies that sell honesty tests. This should not detract from their value, but it is something that needs to be kept in mind as you read them. The low-road strategy where test users are responsible for conducting their own validation studies, and other research as well, is not much in evidence here.

Some mention should be made of topic F in the Introduction to the guidelines, Non-proprietary versus Proprietary Tests. Nearly all honesty tests are proprietary in nature. This means that the scoring keys indicating which responses reflect honesty and which ones reflect dishonesty are held by the publisher and not revealed to the user. Accordingly, scoring is controlled by the publisher. In contrast, non-proprietary tests are sold along with keys and information sufficient so that the user can score and interpret the tests without further reliance on the publisher.

Proprietary testing clearly binds a test user more closely to the publisher on a continuing basis. Its value is that the "right answers" are much less likely to become available to applicants; this type of contamination of test scores is effectively prevented. This is important in honesty testing, where some applicants may well go to considerable lengths to beat the tests. The disadvantage of the proprietary approach is that it places test users in a position of some dependency on the publishers. Furthermore, you cannot make copies of a test on your own once you obtain an original (thus violating copyright laws), because you do not know how to score the test. The test publishers sell pre-numbered tests, and they will only score tests that they have sold.

There was a time when most publishers were wary of those who wanted to have tests scored for any purpose other than direct use by a client. The result was that third-party research on the tests was effectively thwarted. That appears to be no longer true. Most publishers will provide scoring services and tests to qualified researchers, in some instances free of charge. The result has been a substantial growth in the research base of honesty testing. In the long run, this more open policy should increase overall test sales as well.

CONCLUSIONS

We have tried to show how honesty tests are sold and to indicate the competitiveness, and competitive strategies, that characterize this particular marketplace. Critics have been concerned that the ethics of test publishers are not above reproach. We agree with that conclusion. However, for the consumer of honesty tests this simply means that there is a need for greater caution and skepticism. The ultimate response to duplicity in the marketplace is for the user to possess sufficient knowledge to see through the duplicity. Our intent in this book is to provide this type of knowledge. We want you to know enough so you can ask the right questions, and ultimately make the right decisions.

Let us re-emphasize this point. If sales ethics are questionable the solution is not to place the burden of correcting the problem entirely on an upgrading of professional ethics. As attractive as this approach may seem, it will never entirely solve the problem. Sales are often made by non-professionals who are not bound by professional ethics. Professionals can be oblivious to professional pressures. Appeals to professional ethics can even be self-serving in that they reinforce one marketing strategy at the expense of another.

Improved professional ethics are certainly to be desired, but the ultimate solution is a consumer—a test user—who is so informed and knowledgeable that unwarranted and excessive claims simply will not work.

11

The Future of Honesty Testing

In 1989 Michael O'Bannon, Linda Goldinger, and Gavin Appleby concluded their book *Honesty and Integrity Testing: A Practical Guide* with five predictions of future trends. We will use their framework to consider what has transpired since, and to offer our own predictions.

BROADENING OF ADVERTISED FEATURES

The O'Bannon, Goldinger, and Appleby prediction was that scales measuring a variety of characteristics would continue to be incorporated in honesty tests. Thus, more and more tests would yield special scores for employee tenure, drug abuse potential, emotional stability, high productivity, service orientation, work values, hostility, violence potential, and the like.

This procedure is promoted by the prospect that honesty tests may be restricted or prohibited by new legislation. The new scales might survive, whereas omnibus, overt tests for overall honesty would not. Personality-based honesty tests also have this characteristic. They, too, produce multiple scores and provide a hedge against future legislation.

What seems to be happening with honesty tests is not unlike what has already happened with mental ability tests. There are many special ability tests measuring numerical, spatial, mechanical, and a variety of verbal abilities, but there still remain a number of widely used general intelligence tests as well. We think much the same thing will happen with honesty testing.

The special scales that constitute the broadening of advertised features will continue to multiply, and they will dovetail into the varied measures of personality-based honesty tests. Yet to be effective, these special scales will have to be long enough to generate good reliabilities and validities. Many special scales have not had this characteristic in the past, as O'Bannon, Goldinger, and Appleby noted. We believe that longer, more sophisticated special scales will evolve. If, however, employers want to use several of these scales, the testing time required may well become substantial.

Some employers will want the advantages of a battery of special scales covering a range of honesty-related characteristics. They will accept a long testing time to reap these advantages. Nevertheless, there is also a market for relatively short screening devices. These measures of "general honesty" would be expected to be overt tests of the kind that have worked so well to date. Thus we believe the special scales will continue to proliferate, and that test users will be able to select a set of scales to create test batteries for special purposes and jobs. But we also believe that the omnibus, overt tests will also prosper, to be used primarily in situations where theft is the major problem and where, because of high turnover, large numbers of applicants must constantly be screened.

GREATER USAGE OF NEW ADMINISTRATION AND SCORING ALTERNATIVES

O'Bannon, Goldinger, and Appleby predicted that methods of administering honesty tests that extend beyond the traditional paper-and-pencil approach would find greater acceptance. They mention specifically computer administration, audiotapes, videotapes, and automated phone interviews. These types of administration procedures are seeing increasing use within psychological testing generally, and it is not surprising that they have spread to honesty testing.

These approaches increase the size of the market. People who would have difficulty, or in some instances cannot, complete the typical written test are now able to be tested; this includes those with certain disabilities, people whose knowledge of written English is limited, and individuals with low literacy levels. Overall, however, using the new approaches in this way is unlikely to result in a sharp increase in their use. We would expect a slow but steady growth, unless a testing breakthrough occurs that fosters the use of some such approach for everyone. Computerized testing might catch on in this way, but to date it has not. It is best suited to testing situations involving a heavy flow of applicants. Where testing is intermittent, as it is in most company locations, the traditional paper-and-pencil approach is more cost efficient.

Regarding scoring, O'Bannon, Goldinger, and Appleby predict a shift away from proprietary testing, and more use of non-proprietary procedures. We do not see this at present, and are not sure it will occur in the future either. The proprietary approach is very attractive to test publishers because it protects the scoring keys and establishes a continuing close relationship between publisher and user. It also makes it difficult to reproduce the tests and thus avoid paying for them. All in all the proprietary approach appears to offer sufficient advantage to the test publisher, while introducing no major disadvantage for the test user.

Thus, we believe it will remain the dominant scoring approach for the foreseeable future.

INCREASED RESEARCH ACTIVITIES

The prediction of expanded research has proven correct. In fact, the burgeoning of research has moved well beyond what might have been anticipated even five years ago. As is evident from the Bibliography at the end of this book, much of this research has appeared in the *Journal of Business and Psychology*. However, articles have appeared in many other sources as well. A field that until recently was limited largely to the research reports of a few test publishers has spread to become one of the more active research areas in industrial-organizational psychology.

In contrast to a few years ago, this research is being conducted from universities and other sources having no financial relationship to the outcomes. A number of doctoral dissertations related to honesty testing have been carried out. Honesty test publishers are cooperating in these studies, scoring tests for independent researchers. The secrecy that characterized an earlier period seems to have disappeared.

This is important because earlier reviewers of honesty testing research claimed that the studies were so few that meaningful conclusions could not be reached. Whether this was true even then is open to question, but now with so many new studies, a resort to claims that the research is insufficient to justify a conclusion is absurd.

Within this very positive picture we do see some sources of concern, however. The review boards of major journals do not contain many people who have an extensive knowledge of honesty testing. This is not so much because people with this type of knowledge do not exist, as because they are thought to lack the professional stature needed to serve on the review boards. The result is that many reviews are poorly conducted by people who are only tangentially related to the field; good research can be rejected because the reviewers do not have the knowledge to recognize innovative approaches and new ideas. In particular, misperceptions regarding the polygraph and how it can induce confessions tend to stigmatize the review process. We believe that with time these problems will be solved. As honesty testing achieves greater stature, more people with the needed knowledge will exert influence on what is published. But for the moment there is a problem.

GREATER VISIBILITY OF HONESTY TEST PROPONENTS

O'Bannon, Goldinger, and Appleby present evidence that many industry groups and trade associations, even when their members make extensive use of honesty tests, have not endorsed them publicly; they seemed to be deliberately holding back to see what might happen on the legislative front. We cannot claim to be particularly knowledgeable on this score, but we are not aware of a major change in this situation.

There is an area where change has occurred, however, and that change is important. Institutionalized psychology has moved from a lukewarm or even negative position toward honesty tests to a much more positive view. The major impetus has come from the increase in published research and from the meta-analytic reviews. Honesty testing has become a part of the mainstream of personality testing. In the process it has gained substantial support from the psychological community. This movement is still not complete. When it is, we believe that both honesty testing and personality testing overall will have experienced major changes.

FURTHER SCRUTINY OF THE TESTS AND POSSIBILITIES OF NEW LEGISLATION

Clearly the O'Bannon, Goldinger, and Appleby prediction of increased legislation has been confirmed in recent years. The Civil Rights Act of 1991 and the Americans with Disabilities Act have had major impacts on honesty testing. Much of this influence has been achieved because of the ambiguity inherent in the legislation. Future court interpretations or new legislation may reverse this. Nevertheless, the consequences of recent federal legislation, and some state legislation as well, cannot be denied. Over the past five years honesty testing has suffered some setbacks.

Can we expect this trend to continue into the future? At the federal level we believe there is little immediate prospect of further restrictive change. The shift in the national political climate away from liberal ideologies to a more pro-business climate, and thus the reduced support for new social legislation, should provide some respite from the attack on honesty testing. Labor unions have often been at the forefront of the anti-honesty testing movement, and at the moment they are not in a position to have a major impact on legislation. Thus we see little likelihood of federal honesty testing legislation in the short term. Nevertheless, a shift in the political climate could signal change in the future.

At the state level the situation is more volatile. Honesty test publishers and users are becoming more active at this level, which should serve to head off a burst of restrictive legislation. To date, we do not see the rapid escalation of state activity that served to spark other kinds of federal social legislation. Yet state support of privacy actions could produce a more restrictive legal climate, even without direct legislative enactments. Overall, we do not believe the states, any more than the federal government, will introduce major restrictions on honesty testing. We hesitate to say that the coast is clear, but it certainly is clearer than it was a few years ago.

CONCLUSIONS

O'Bannon, Goldinger, and Appleby conclude their discussion by saying, "The future of honesty and integrity testing is likely to involve the same type of hurdles which faced the polygraph industry.'' Whether the tests will clear these hurdles or be stymied by them remains to be seen.

We believe that now the polygraph analogy is much less relevant for honesty testing. The honesty test story has not played out along the same lines as the polygraph model would suggest. Accordingly, we foresee a prosperous future for honesty testing. These tests serve a significant need. It is important that they be permitted to continue to serve that need, and we believe that society will have the good sense to let that happen.

Appendix: Development and Validation of an Honesty Test

As noted in the Introduction, we have had considerable experience working together in the honesty testing industry. The results of our research are noted at various places in this book to illustrate points we wish to make.

Chapter 3 includes some findings from our research validating the test against a polygraph criterion (see Table 3.1). It also reports on a contrasted group validation study which utilized prisoners in comparison with job applicants (see Figure 3.1). A pilot study looking into comparisons against inventory shrinkage is discussed as well.

Chapter 4 offers data on the extent to which our test results were influenced by the educational level of those who took the tests (see Table 4.1).

Chapter 5 presents information on the test-retest reliability of our measure (see Table 5.1). It also deals with the matter of item selection and how we did it. Data are presented on whether respondents found our questionnaire items to be offensive, and thus potentially invasive of privacy (see Table 5.2). Finally, we provide figures derived from a special scale designed to pick up random responding or distortions of other kinds (see Table 5.3).

Chapter 6 deals with establishing cutting scores and presents data from our research showing how this may be done (see Table 6.1). It also contains a discussion of the false positive issue, illustrated with findings from our validation research.

Chapter 7 considers adverse impact and shows how the four-fifths rule may be applied (see Table 7.1). It also considers adverse impact as it may manifest itself in company hiring. The passage of the Civil Rights Act of 1991 occasioned a shift in the scoring procedures for our test from one based on scoring differentiated by race and sex to a single undifferentiated score. This change had substantial impact (see Table 7.2).

Chapter 8 covers our experience subsequent to the passage of the Americans with Disabilities Act (ADA). It details at length the legal dilemmas we faced as the law went into effect. The discussion provides numerous examples of the legal concerns that the ADA introduced.

The illustrations sprinkled throughout the various chapters are intended to help make certain points we wish to emphasize. At no point has there been an integrated presentation of our research program. Yet certain readers may wish to have a better understanding of how we developed our scoring systems, how we validated them, and what we learned from our research. The following presentation overlaps to some degree with what has been said previously. It does not deal with everything contained in the prior chapters. It is intended rather as a technical presentation of test development and validation considerations only—much like a journal article. Many readers will have little interest in this kind of integrated statement of our research program; a few will feel a strong need to fill in the blanks between the intermittent discussions spaced throughout the book. To meet the needs of these varied readers we have (1) prepared a presentation of our research, and (2) relegated the discussion to an appendix so as not to impose it on those with little interest in it.

The review of measures of honesty and integrity by the American Psychological Association task force, consisting of Lewis Goldberg, Julia Grenier, Robert Guion, Lee Sechrest, and Hilda Wing (1991), notes seven basic approaches used in validity studies. Two of these form the focus of this report. They are described by the task force as follows:

Contrasted groups. For example, the attitudes of convicted felons have been compared with those of nonfelons in regard to theft, violence, and illicit drug use.

Comparison with polygraph performance. Because some businesses that previously used the polygraph for pre-employment screening now use honesty tests for the same purpose, it is probably only natural that one form of test validation is the demonstration that the two procedures produce similar results. (p. 15)

The use of these approaches has not gone without challenge. The report on the subject by the Office of Technology Assessment of the U.S. Congress (1990) questions the construct equivalence of honesty and integrity as they operate in normal job applicants and convicted felons, and rejects completely the use of polygraph performance on the grounds that the validity of this criterion has never been demonstrated. Yet as Ones, Viswesvaran, and Schmidt (1993) explicitly point out, correlations with polygraph results and comparisons of criminal and non-criminal samples are useful for purposes of studying construct validity.

Comprehensive reviews of the honesty and integrity testing literature cite many more studies utilizing polygraph performance as a criterion than studies using contrasted groups involving convicted criminals (Jones, 1991a; Sackett and Harris, 1984; Sackett, Burris, and Callahan, 1989). However, there have been few studies with the polygraph in the past 10 years. Furthermore, much of the research on both subjects has been reported in sources other than formal scientific publications—unpublished papers given at meetings, test publishers' technical reports, and the like. One reason for the paucity of published research in these areas is that the studies are often flawed in one way or another, and thus do not meet the criteria for journal publication (O'Bannon, Goldinger, and Appleby, 1989; Sackett, Burris, and Callahan, 1989; Murphy, 1993).

It is also true that the flaws vary from one study to another, while the results exhibit considerable consistency. The weight of the evidence thus suggests that various measures of honesty do relate to polygraph performance, and that those who have been convicted of various crimes do score at a low level on these measures. The objective of our research was to attempt to confirm these findings, while keeping the flaws to a minimum, and to investigate factors associated with the underlying honesty construct.

The instrument used in these studies was originally developed using an item-selection procedure that relied on relationships with polygraph performance as a criterion. A similar tie to the polygraph appears to underlie the development of many clear-purpose honesty tests currently on the market (Ash, 1991).

STUDY 1: USING A DIFFERENTIATED SCORING SYSTEM

Measures

The test instrument utilized in these studies remained the same throughout; however, various scoring systems have been used. The test includes 82 items. The initial selection of items and development of the scoring systems utilized groups differentiated by race and sex, and thus incorporated the study of differences associated with these factors from the outset. To our knowledge, no previous honesty testing study has done this. The basic procedure was to establish extreme groups of 50 job applicants who had clearly passed a polygraph evaluation and 50 who had clearly failed (leaving out the more ambiguous middle ground). Then item responses were computed separately for both extreme groups, and if any difference between groups in the percentage selecting a particular response was identified, weights were assigned (a 6–15 percent difference having a weight of 1, 16–26 having a weight of 2, and so on.). Criterion groups were established separately for black females, white females, black males, and white males. Thus, any analysis of an item pool contained 400 people, each in one of eight criterion groups. Then the results were cross validated in a combined sample containing representatives of all four criterion groups. This sample represented a straight run of 100 job candidates as they became available (and thus contained all levels of polygraph evaluations, including the more ambiguous middle ground previously excluded).

To clarify, and because there have been some problems in making this entirely clear, what we did is compare:

50 black women who passed the polygraph with 50 black women who did not

50 black men who passed the polygraph with 50 black men who did not

50 white women who passed the polygraph with 50 white women who did not

50 white men who passed the polygraph with 50 white men who did not

Then the items that produced responses differentiating people who passed the polygraph from those who did not were incorporated in a test which was administered to:

100 new individuals of both races and sexes who covered the full range of polygraph performance

Assuming that this cross validation with 100 new cases produced significant results, items were selected for the final test to the extent that they yielded larger item weights and to the extent that they yielded weights at all across a larger number of the four sets of criterion samples (black and white, women and men). Two rounds of item selection were carried out, which resulted in the selection of the final 82 items from an original pool totaling 137. Thus, the procedure just described was carried out again in its entirety (500 new subjects taking both honesty test items and polygraph), but using a completely new set of items.

The items themselves were of two major types. One type consisted of scenario items, an example of which would be the following:

Jane works as a sales clerk in the store beside the Interstate Highway. The store's customers are mostly tourists who stop by to buy gasoline, snacks, and souvenirs. One day Jane accidentally gives a man change for a $10 bill when he actually had given her a $20 bill. After the man left, Jane saw the $20 bill in the cash drawer with the tens and realized what she had done. At this point Jane might react in several ways. Indicate whether you agree with each of these possibilities.

1. Jane decides to deny that she shortchanged the customer if he returns for his $10. That will save her a lot of embarrassment. Do you agree?
   Yes _____ No _____

2. Jane regrets the incident, but decides to make the best of a bad situation. She takes $10 from the cash drawer and tells her supervisor she is sick and wants the rest of the day off. Do you agree?
   Yes _____ No _____

3. Jane will gladly return the $10 to the customer if she sees him again. Meanwhile, she turns the extra money over to the store manager and decides to make up for the mistake by contributing $10 of her own money to a local charity. Do you agree?
   Yes _____ No _____

4. Jane turns the extra money over to the store at the end of her shift because the customer has not returned. She also writes down everything she can remember about how the man looks. If he ever stops at the store again, she will repay him with her

own money. Do you agree?

Yes _____   No _____

All such scenario items were placed in Part I of the test. In most cases there were four Yes-No questions following each scenario, although in one instance 10 questions were appended to the same scenario. The final test contained 54 items of this type (12 scenarios). Part II of the test contained 28 items of a kind more typically used in overt honesty tests. These involved confessions to cheating or lying, rationalization of dishonest behavior, and outright confessions to criminal behavior or conviction. Examples are the following:

If I saw a person accidentally throw away a winning ticket at a race track, I would hand it back to that person.

Yes _____   No _____

If I got caught stealing, I think I should be given another chance if it was the first time it ever happened.

Yes _____   No _____

Have you cheated on the number of hours you have worked for any employer?

Yes _____   No _____

The item-weighting process operated as follows: utilizing for purposes of illustration, say, the black female samples:

	Responses in the sample of those who passed the polygraph		**Responses in the sample of those who failed the polygraph**	
	Yes	No	Yes	No
Percent	90	10	72	28

In this instance the apparently more honest response was Yes and it was selected 18 percent more frequently. Thus, the Yes response was given a weight of 2 among black females. In other race-sex groups the weight could be different, and it could even be that the No response received the positive weight, if those who passed the polygraph had a higher percentage value for No than those who failed. This item-weighting procedure is discussed by Robert Guion (1965) and was utilized, for example, by Edwin Ghiselli (1971) in developing his Self-Description Inventory.

The score for an individual whose characteristics placed him or her in a particular race-sex group was the sum of the weights for all items on which the respondent selected the response more characteristic of those who passed the polygraph in that group. The maximum number of scorable items (receiving some weight) using this differentiated scoring system was 58 for black females (Part I 34 and Part II 24), 60 for black males (Part I 36 and Part II 24), 47 for white females (Part I 26 and Part II 21), and 59 for white males (Part I 35 and

Part II 24). To equalize the scores of different groups, standard scores were computed, setting the mean for each race-sex group at 50 and the standard deviation equal to 10. This procedure served to preclude finding any race or sex differences in the normative sample used to compute the standard scores.

The polygraph measures used to establish criterion groups, and in all other analyses, were obtained using trained examiners, who administered the examinations for client companies to assist them in making hiring decisions. These examiners completed a standard form dealing with such matters as occupational history, health, criminal activity, alcohol and drug use, gambling, debts, and the like based on the responses of the job applicants during the polygraph examination. These forms were in turn scored by Michael Capps, an experienced polygraph examiner and instructor, using the following scale:

1. No marijuana use in the past year; no hard drug use ever; no drug sales, no convictions; no serious undetected crime; no theft of money from any previous employer, no theft of more than $20 in merchandise per year from any previous employer, no single item of more than $5; no current alcohol problem.

2. Has used marijuana in the last year, but not on a weekly basis; has not used hard drugs within the last year; has not sold drugs ever; no convictions, no serious undetected crimes; no money theft from previous employer; no theft of merchandise of more than $100 per year, or no single item of $10 or more from any previous employer; no current alcohol problem.

3. Uses marijuana no more than twice a week; has smoked marijuana on the job but not in the last year. Has used hard drugs, but not in the last year; used cocaine less than once a month; has stolen money from a previous employer, but less than $20 in a year; has stolen merchandise from a previous employer, but less than $200 in a year.

4. Uses marijuana four or five days a week; used marijuana on the last job, or on the current job; has used hard drugs within the past year; uses cocaine on a monthly basis; has stolen more than $20 in money in a year from some previous employer; has stolen more than $200 in merchandise in a year from some previous employer; has been convicted of a felony or of other crimes involving theft, or had attitudinal problems which would have a bearing on the job; participation in crimes of a like nature in which the person was not caught.

The criterion samples contained individuals who scored 4 on the polygraph (failed) and individuals who scored 1 or in a few instances at the 2 level on either theft or drug use but not both (passed). Honesty or integrity test items were administered before or after the polygraph depending on the availability of the examiners.

Samples and Analyses

Normative Sample. This sample contains 67,405 cases whose test records came to a centralized scoring center over a three-year period. These were job applicants distributed throughout the United States, being evaluated by a wide range of client companies. In general they were applying for jobs that were not at a high skill level, that tended to concentrate in retailing, and that involved considerable customer contact. There were 9,389 black females, 21,781 white females, 12,091 black males, and 24,144 white males.

Polygraph Sample. This was a new sample of 100 consecutive cases whose test records became available in conjunction with polygraph reports. The polygraph scores were at all levels (1, 2, 3, and 4). This sample was similar to the two groups of 100 used in selecting items for the test; however, these subjects completed the full 82-item version. This sample contained 19 black females, 17 white females, 20 black males, and 44 white males. The sample was used to obtain an estimate of test validity by correlating the scores with polygraph results; it is a cross-validation sample.

Reliability Sample. Members of this sample completed the test twice to provide an index of test-retest reliability. This appears to be the appropriate approach to estimating test reliability in instances such as this (Cortina, 1993). There were 62 cases in the sample—13 black females, 15 white females, 21 black males, and 13 white males. They were applicants for positions with a wide range of employers. The mean interval between testings was 30 days. However, this figure is heavily influenced by several extreme cases, with 11 percent of the intervals extending beyond 100 days. In contrast, 61 percent of the sample was retested within a week.

Prison Sample. These were 117 prisoners incarcerated in five different prisons in the State of Georgia. Among the 93 males, 46 were in a maximum security prison, 10 were in a moderate security institution, 18 were in a minimum security facility, and 19 were in a youthful offender prison housing certified juvenile incorrigibles. The 24 females were all from a single women's facility. There were 11 black females, 13 white females, 40 black males, and 53 white males.

The prisoners were volunteers and were selected insofar as possible to include a number of property offenders; at least 91 percent of the cases were of this type. The prisoners were instructed to complete the test as they would if they were applying for a job. Prisoners believed to possess a reading level below seventh grade were excluded, since that was the reading level of the test. Comparisons were made between the test scores obtained in the prison sample and those of the normative sample.

Matched Sample. Because Part I and Part II scores were not available separately for the normative sample as a whole, a similar sample reflecting the total score distribution of the normative sample was created. The objective was to compare part scores, and thus different types of items. Like the prison sample, this group of job applicants from the normative sample contained 11 black females, 13 white females, 40 black males, and 53 white males. Mean scores for the total test, and for each of the two parts separately, were compared with those for the prison sample.

Table A.1
Validity against Polygraph Results in a Sample of Job Applicants, and Test-Retest Reliabilities, Using the Differentiated Scoring System

Test Scores	Validity (N=100) r	Reliability (N=62) r
Total Score (Standardized)	0.69**	0.98**
Part I Score	0.49**	0.88**
Part II Score	0.48**	0.94**

**$p < 0.01$

Balanced Sample. The balanced sample was created to study the relationships among the four differentiated scoring systems. The sample consisted of 25 black females, 25 white females, 25 black males, and 25 white males. These 100 job applicants were scored on all four scales. One of these scores is the appropriate one for the person, and three are not. Scores were calculated separately for Parts I and II and for the whole test. Correlations among the four scores, with the appropriateness of the scoring system held constant, indicate whether the differentiated scoring system serves a useful purpose.

A second approach to this question utilized the actual scores (weights) for each item in the four scoring systems, rather than the scored tests used in the balanced sample. In this approach, the Part I correlations were based on 54 items, the Part II correlations on 28, and the total score correlations on 82. Yes responses in a scoring system were given a plus value, with the appropriate weight, and No responses a minus value. Where no weight was assigned for an item, it was scored zero. The numbers of entries were 54, 28, and 82, respectively. The correlations provide a measure of the comparability of the four scales.

Results

Table A.1 contains the validity coefficients obtained in the polygraph sample. In this analysis, 36 percent of the subjects passed the polygraph and 64 percent were questionable or did not pass. Applying this same ratio to the total test scores, 24 percent of the cases pass both the test and the polygraph, 51 percent fail both, and 25 percent are off-quadrant ($\chi^2 = 21.32$, $p < 0.01$).

It is apparent that both Part I and Part II item types contribute approximately equally to the results. The two parts do not correlate significantly. Overall, the validity obtained is high compared with reports of results obtained with other tests (Sackett, Burris, and Callahan, 1989). However, the explicit way in which item selection and weighting was tied to the polygraph, plus the use of differentiated scoring, clearly contributes to this result. Also, validity coefficients at

Figure A.1
Prison and Normative Samples Compared Using Differentiated Scoring

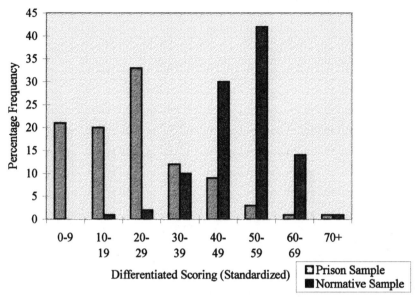

this level have been obtained in other studies conducted outside the honesty testing context (Miner, Ebrahimi, and Wachtel, 1995; Miner, Smith, and Bracker, 1994).

The data from the reliability analysis in Table A.1 indicate entirely adequate findings. Overall, these correlations are high among reported test-retest reliabilities (Sackett, Burris, and Callahan, 1989). There are no significant differences between means at first test and retest.

Figure A.1 contrasts the test scores in the prison sample with those in the normative sample. It is apparent that the prisoners score substantially below job applicants. In the low score range, where employability is minimal (standard scores of 0 to 39), one finds 86 percent of the prisoners and only 13 percent of the normative sample. In the moderate to very high employability range (standard scores of 40 and above), there are only 14 percent of the prisoners and 87 percent of the job applicants.

Table A.2 compares the prison sample and the matched sample. The scores in the latter are substantially higher. This appears to be due almost entirely to the Part II results. Note that the matched sample standard score mean is indeed almost exactly at 50 and the standard deviation at 10. Thus, the desired matching to the normative sample was achieved. The Part I difference is in the anticipated direction, favoring the matched sample, but is not sufficient to yield significance. What we can say with certainty from this analysis is that the Part II score contributes disproportionately to the results. Beyond this it should be noted that

Table A.2
Comparisons of Mean Scores for Prison and Matched Samples Using the
Differentiated Scoring System

Test Scores	Prison Sample (N=117)		Matched Sample (N=117)		
	M	SD	M	SD	t
Total Score					
(Standardized)	22.22	15.45	49.96	10.15	16.23**
Part I Score	23.42	5.31	24.40	5.03	1.45
Part II Score	5.53	13.61	29.97	6.91	17.31**

$*p < 0.05$
$**p < 0.01$

responses to items involving confessions to convictions or criminal behavior within Part II indicate a 97 percent confession rate in the prison sample and an 11 percent confession rate in the matched sample. Clearly, confessions are a major factor discriminating prisoners from job applicants.

When the standard score distributions for the prison and matched samples are compared, the results are almost identical to those in Figure A.1. The chi-square value is 144.48 ($p < 0.01$; df = 6).

Within the prison sample, the white males prove to have lower total test scores (standardized) than the other race-sex groups ($F = 7.83$, $p < 0.01$). The white male mean is 15.23, in contrast with 29.18 for the black females, 28.23 for the white females, and 27.63 for the black males. No significant difference is apparent when the mean scores for the five prison types are compared ($F = 1.63$), although the lowest scores derive from the maximum security prison, and the highest from the women's facility.

Table A.3 presents the results from comparisons of the four differentiated scoring systems with one another using the balanced sample scores and the actual scores (weights) inherent in the items of the systems themselves. In general, these two approaches yield similar results. The total score correlations have a median value overall of 0.38 (with 0.38 for the actual scores and 0.30 for the scored tests). The Part I score correlations yield a median of −0.06 overall (with 0.02 for the actual scores and −0.06 for the scored tests). The Part II median correlation is 0.67 (with 0.65 for the actual scores and 0.72 for the scored tests).

The pattern that emerges from this analysis varies little with the analytic approach used. The Part I (scenario) items contribute most to the differentiated scoring; here the scoring systems for various race-sex groups are on the average totally unrelated. The black females and black males do yield some evidence of a positive relationship, but other than that all significant relationships are negative.

Table A.3

Intercorrelations among Scoring Systems Using the Scores Obtained in a Balanced Sample (N = 100) and the Actual Scores for Items Derived from Item Analysis

	Scoring System Used							
	Black Female		Black Male		White Female		White Male	
	Actual Scores	Scored Tests	Actual Scores	Scored Tests	Actual Scores	Scored Tests	Actual Scores	Scored Tests
Total Scores								
Black Female	—	—	0.39**	0.65**	0.33**	0.39**	0.38**	0.18
Black Male			—	—	0.38**	0.49**	0.62**	0.20*
White Female					—	—	0.31**	-0.07
White Male							—	—
Part I Scores								
Black Female	—	—	0.20	0.51**	-0.13	-0.01	0.16	-0.10
Black Male			—	—	-0.28*	0.04	0.26	-0.26**
White Female					—	—	-0.39**	-0.45**
White Male							—	—
Part II Scores								
Black Female	—	—	0.37*	0.79**	0.69**	0.82**	0.40*	0.62**
Black Male			—	—	0.73**	0.82**	0.73**	0.64**
White Female					—	—	0.60**	0.62**
White Male							—	—

$*p < 0.05$
$**p < 0.01$

In contrast Part II, made up of items more traditional to the honesty testing field, produces correlations among the differentiated scores sufficiently high that differential scoring is probably not needed. In several cases the scoring system intercorrelations come close to the reliability of 0.94 for Part II reported in Table A.1. If there is any evidence of differentiation it is because the white males are slightly less similar to the other three groups than those groups are to one another.

Given these sharp differences between the findings with Part I and Part II scores, the total score results have relatively little meaning. They simply represent the interaction of these two disparate influences.

If the mean scores across the four scoring systems derived from the item selection and weighting process are compared, the total score means ranged from -0.17 for the white males to -0.83 for the black males, with -0.52 for the white females and -0.61 for the black females. All of these scores indicate a predominance of No responses, with $F = 2.99$, $p < 0.05$, however. The white males were significantly less negative than the black males. This total score difference was attributable only to the Part I scores. There, with $F = 4.06$, $p < 0.01$, the white males had a mean score of 0.31 in the Yes direction, while the black males with a score of -0.33 and the black females with a score of -0.31 both differed significantly with scores in the No direction. The white female mean was -0.20. In Part II there were no significant differences ($F = 1.04$), and scores ranged from -1.07 for white males to -1.76 for black males. These results serve to emphasize the fact that the scoring systems are in fact distinct, using a different approach. Yet the differences appear to closely parallel those produced by the correlational analysis.

STUDY 2: USING AN UNDIFFERENTIATED SCORING SYSTEM

The findings of this second study would never have emerged had it not been for the passage of the Civil Rights Act of 1991. In an attempt to limit race norming of the General Aptitude Test Battery, the U.S. Congress incorporated a paragraph on that subject in the Act. This paragraph reads as follows:

It shall be an unlawful employment practice for a respondent, in connection with the selection or referral of applicants or candidates for employment or promotion, to adjust the scores of, use different cutoff scores for, or otherwise alter the results of, employment related tests on the basis of race, color, religion, sex, or national origin.

Although the true implications of this paragraph for honesty tests remain elusive, there was reason to believe that the differentiated scoring system might well be illegal. Accordingly, a single, undifferentiated procedure which could be used with all race and sex groups was developed. This procedure should be more like other overt honesty tests. Thus, there was an opportunity to compare the results obtained in Study 1 with the results of a more traditional type of measurement.

Measures

The test used in Study 2 was the same as that used in Study 1. What differed was the scoring system. The initial step in developing an undifferentiated scoring system was to go back to the data of Study 1 in which comparisons were made between samples of 50 each, with one sample containing those who clearly passed the polygraph and the other containing those who clearly failed. The objective now was to identify items within the test that produced the highest *average* discrimination between honest and dishonest respondents (as defined by the polygraph). This average discrimination statistic was calculated for the normative sample as a whole.

Once this difference measure was obtained, it was used in exactly the same way as the race-sex group difference measures were used in Study 1. If the value was 5 or less, the item was not scored. If it was 6–15, a weight of 1 was given to either the Yes or No response depending on which predominated in the pass (or honest) group. If it was 16–25, a weight of 2 was given, and so on. As might be expected from the data in Table A.3, this procedure resulted in a number of previously scorable items being eliminated. Differences in opposite directions in two different groups would cancel each other out. As anticipated, item loss was most pronounced in Part I of the test.

This scoring system contained 41 scorable items of the 82 in the test. In contrast, the differentiated scoring system for the black female, black male, white female, and white male groups produced a score for one or more of the groups on 77 items of the 82. Part I of the test now contained only 15 scorable items, all with the minimum possible weight of 1. In Study 1, 49 of these items were used in some manner, and there were numerous weights of 2 and 3. In contrast, Part II contributed 26 scorable items to the undifferentiated measure, down only slightly from the 28 tapped by one or more of the differentiated measures. This result is consistent with the pattern of correlations in Table A.3.

Samples and Analyses

Normative Sample. This was the same sample as used in Study 1, except that Hispanic males and females could appropriately be included using the undifferentiated scoring system, and consequently the N was increased to 70,950.

Polygraph Sample. This was the cross-validation sample from Study 1. Accordingly, direct comparisons could be made between the differentiated and undifferentiated scoring systems.

Reliability Sample. This, too, was the sample from Study 1, thus permitting direct comparisons between the two approaches to scoring.

Table A.4

Validity against Polygraph Results in a Sample of Job Applicants, and Test-Retest Reliabilities, Using the Undifferentiated Scoring System

Test Scores	Validity (*N*=100) r	Reliability (*N*=62) r
Total Score	0.62**	0.80**
Part I Score	0.01	0.64**
Part II Score	0.61	0.87**

**p < 0.01

Prison Sample. Again, the sample used in Study 1 was utilized. Comparisons were made on the same basis.

Matched Sample. This sample, too, remained the same. In addition to the analyses made in Study 1, it was used to determine the relationship between the differentiated and undifferentiated scoring systems.

The balanced sample was not used in Study 2. However, correlations were calculated between actual scores (weights) used in the undifferentiated system and the actual scores of the four differentiated approaches as used in Table A.3.

Results

Table A.4 gives the validity coefficients obtained in the polygraph sample. With the shift to undifferentiated scoring, validity drops from 0.69 to 0.62, but it remains quite high. The major change, however, is that Part I loses all validity, while Part II assumes the entire predictive burden. The loss of scorable items in Part I, with the result that the standard deviation of Part I scores is only 1.57, eliminates any correlation with the polygraph results.

When the 36 percent pass and 64 percent fail ratio is applied to both the test scores and the polygraph results, 22 percent of the cases pass both measures, 50 percent fail both, and 28 percent are off quadrant ($\chi^2 = 15.25$, $p < 0.01$). Thus, the undifferentiated scoring produces only a very small decrement in predictive effectiveness.

The reliability data provided in Table A.4 indicate that the undifferentiated scoring system is less reliable than the differentiated system. The decrease in scorable items within Part I appears to have produced a sharp decrease in test-retest reliability there. Part II reliability holds up reasonably well, but the net effect is a substantial drop in total score correlations. Presumably, this decrease in reliability is the cause of the decreased validity. There continues to be no difference between first test and retest mean scores.

Figure A.2 contrasts the prison sample scores with those of the normative sample. The results approximate those of Figure A.1. In the low score range,

Figure A.2
Prison and Normative Samples Compared Using Undifferentiated Scoring

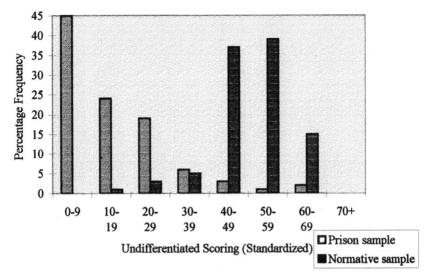

where employability is minimal—with standard scores of 0 to 39—we find 94 percent of the prisoners and only 9 percent of the normative group. In the moderate to very high employability range, where standard scores are 40 and above, only 6 percent of the prisoners are found, and 91 percent of the job applicants.

Table A.5 provides data on the comparisons between the prison and matched samples. In all instances, the prison data are significantly, and substantially, lower. Particularly important is the fact that, in contrast to the findings of Table A.4, Part I now yields a significant result. This is also in contrast to the findings of Table A.2. It appears that in a somewhat different validation context, the depleted Part I score still can work. Yet the Part II difference, with its major confession component, works best.

Again, when the prison and matched sample score distributions are compared, the results very closely approximate those of Figure A.2. The chi-square value is 176.26 ($p < 0.01$, df $= 6$).

Table A.6 contains information on race-sex group differences within the prison sample. As in Study 1, the white males have distinctly lower scores, and it is now possible to attribute this to the Part II results. It also appears that the scores from the maximum security prison are lower on Part II, as one might expect. This raises a question as to whether the low scores of the white males might not be associated with a greater likelihood of their being in the maximum security prison. This turns out to be the case. While 65 percent of the prisoners from the maximum security institution are white males, white males represent only 45 percent of the prison sample as a whole.

Table A.5
Comparisons of Mean Scores for Prison and Matched Samples Using the
Undifferentiated Scoring System

Test Scores	Prison Sample (N=117)		Matched Sample (N=117)		t
	M	SD	M	SD	
Total Score	14.30	10.46	34.91	5.33	18.99**
Part I Score	8.29	1.91	9.90	1.71	6.78**
Part II Score	6.03	10.09	25.01	5.37	17.95**

*$p < 0.05$
**$p < 0.01$

In the matched sample, which has been selected to directly model the normative sample, and which accordingly should provide the most representative results, the correlation between differentiated and undifferentiated scores is 0.74 ($p < 0.01$). The two scoring systems are not the same, but they appear to measure similar constructs in much the same way that different intelligence tests do.

Table A.7 provides information on the relationships between undifferentiated scoring and the various differentiated scores in the same way that Table A.3 does for the various differentiated scores. Note that the total score correlations are consistently significant and high. The Part II correlations consistently exceed the total score values, and the Part I correlations are consistently below them, even to the point of in one instance failing to obtain significance. Clearly, Part I is not a major component of the undifferentiated system, although it does yield validity in comparisons involving the prison sample.

DISCUSSION AND CONCLUSIONS

It is apparent that the test proves more often than not to be a valid measure of honesty based on polygraph comparisons and comparisons with prisoner status. The major point to be made in this regard is not that this particular measure works for this purpose, but that prior findings to this effect are confirmed with a completely independent measure. Thus, evidence for construct validity is added.

The results presented in Study 1 and the implication of the Study 2 findings lead to the conclusion that honesty may well show substantial variations from one race-sex group to another. If this is true, valid measurement would require that these variations be reflected in the measures used (see Scientific Affairs Committee, 1993). This, in turn, would raise serious questions regarding a pos-

Table A.6

Comparisons of Mean Scores for Race-Sex Groupings and Prison Types Using the Undifferentiated Scoring System

Test Scores	Race-Sex Grouping				
	Black Females	Black Males	White Females	White Males	F
Total Scores	17.55	16.38	19.23	10.85	4.06**
Part I Scores	7.55	7.83	8.69	8.64	1.96
Part II Scores	10.00	8.55	10.54	2.21	5.33**

	Prison Type					
	Minimum Security	Moderate Security	Maximum Security	Women's Facility	Youthful Offenders	F
Total Scores	15.11	16.60	11.33	18.46	14.26	2.10
Part I Scores	8.50	7.50	8.35	8.17	8.36	.56
Part II Scores	6.61	9.10	2.98	10.29	5.90	2.49*

*$p < 0.05$
**$p < 0.01$

sible conflict between certain provisions of the Civil Rights Act of 1991 in the area of race and sex norming and the requirements for a business necessity defense. We have presented evidence that some such differentiation with regard to honesty exists, but have said nothing as to the specific nature of this differentiation.

This can only be established by analyzing those responses that differentiate the various race-sex groups. Study 2 cannot contribute directly to this goal, but Study 1 can. Our approach was to abstract out of the test data what the respondents were saying when the members of one group responded differently from the members of another (i.e., selected Yes disproportionately more than No, or No more than Yes). In short, we looked specifically at items (almost always in Part I) where honesty (passing the polygraph) was associated with one response in one group and the opposite in another (i.e., the items which differentiated). Furthermore, we looked only at responses that carried a weight of 2 or more. Items with weight 1 might be useful for statistical purposes, but they carry too much noise for purposes of item interpretation. The interpretations accordingly are based on relatively few items, but items that carry clearer information—7 for black females, 11 for black males, 10 for white females, and 9 for white males. Honesty for this purpose was originally defined by the polygraph results, but it was strongly supported by the prison results as well.

Table A.7

Correlations between the Undifferentiated Scores and Differentiated Scores for Various Race-Sex Groups Using the Actual Scores for Items Derived from the Item Analysis

Undifferentiated Scoring System	Differentiated Scoring System			
	Black Females	Black Males	White Females	White Males
Total Scores	0.57**	0.70**	0.66**	0.84**
Part I Scores	0.35**	0.38**	0.14	0.63**
Part II Scores	0.65**	0.76**	0.86**	0.88**

*$p < 0.05$
**$p < 0.01$

The honest black females, as opposed to the dishonest, tend to portray themselves as less likely to cheat and lie themselves, but also as less disposed to become involved where others exhibit dishonest behavior. To a disproportionate extent they tend to favor punishing those who deserve it.

The honest black males, as opposed to the dishonest, tend actually to portray themselves as more disposed to engage in dishonest behavior under certain circumstances. They are more likely to say that they could become involved in activities where they cheat or lie, they are more likely to believe that some type of dishonesty is justified, and they are disproportionately disposed to rationalize dishonest behaviors in others on occasion. It is possible that what is involved here is a greater tendency to be truthful about their feelings.

The honest white females, as opposed to the dishonest, tend to portray themselves as less likely to cheat or engage in dishonest behavior. At the same time they indicate less of a tendency to report dishonesty in others, especially friends, and have a greater preference not to involve others or talk to others when a situation presents temptations. There seems to be a greater overall sensitivity to interpersonal factors in the context of dishonesty, with the result that they are more likely to feel that punishment for dishonest behavior may not be justified. This pattern is similar to the female leadership style identified by Eagly and Johnson (1990).

The honest white males, as opposed to the dishonest, tend to portray themselves as people who in general would not lie, cheat, and steal; who try to avoid temptations; and who would report dishonesty in others. Yet there are situations where they are particularly likely to feel some dishonesty may be justified. Overall, one gets the impression that conventional conceptions of honesty and integrity are more closely allied with the white male pattern than any of the others.

These differentiated patterns are, of course, derived from post hoc analyses.

They are not proven findings, but hypotheses for further study. Nevertheless, they do appear to be worth studying. The problem of defining honest respondents has been made more difficult by the passage of the Polygraph Protection Act. Yet the finding that contrasted groups yield much the same result as the polygraph does appear to offer a way out. In particular, it might be valuable to study the test item responses of people who have been cleared of any dishonesty through a thorough background investigation and contrast them with responses from a prison population. Although we appear to have a good idea of how to predict dishonest behavior (see Ones, Viswesvaran, and Schmidt, 1993), we know little about why or when we can predict. We do know now, however, that the underlying construct is differentiated by sex and race, and that item type is an important consideration in this differentiation.

A factor distinguishing the test responses of prisoners, and those with failing polygraph scores, from the test responses of job applicants in general and those with passing polygraph scores is the degree to which confessions are present in the test responses. This is significant for several reasons. It brings into serious question the contention that prisoners will not confess to crimes because they believe this might jeopardize their parole chances (Sackett and Harris, 1984). Prisoners clearly do confess, but so, too, do job applicants, especially those job applicants who do poorly on the polygraph. But in our experience, a high proportion of job applicants who fail the polygraph do so because they confess to a crime.

In short, the evidence available to us suggests that the polygraph and honesty or integrity tests may work for much the same reasons—they tend to elicit confessions. We recognize the tendency recently for honesty test publishers to distance themselves from the polygraph (Association of Personnel Test Publishers, 1991; Sackett, Burris, and Callahan, 1989). Nevertheless, the evidence is not easily ignored.

In the hiring situation, polygraph examiners typically attempt to convince job applicants that the device can see through their defenses and determine whether they are telling the truth (Bashore and Rapp, 1993). In many cases this may not even be necessary: the applicants bring an assumption of omniscience to the examination. Faced with this situation, and believing that they will be found out anyway, many applicants confess to something. They may not confess to everything they could, they may try to cast their confessions in a favorable light or minimize the extent of their guilt, but they confess. It seems very likely that most clear-purpose honesty tests operate in exactly the same manner. Here, omniscience is attributed to the psychologists who develop the tests, not to a polygraph examiner, but the net effect is the same. The tests are assumed to possess some ingenious method of entering into a person's mind, and to the extent this assumption is firmly in place, the tests do exactly that.

Bibliography

Allen, Jeffrey G. *Complying with the ADA: A Small Business Guide to Hiring and Employing the Disabled.* New York: John Wiley & Sons, 1993.

American Psychiatric Association. *Diagnostic and Statistical Manual of Mental Disorders*, 4th ed. (DSM-IV). Washington, D.C., 1994.

Anfuso, Dawn. Deflecting Workplace Violence. *Personnel Journal*, Volume 73, Number 10 (October 1994), pp. 66–77.

Armstrong-Stassen, Marjorie and Judith W. Tansky. Personality Correlates of Two Integrity Tests. Working paper, University of Windsor, 1995.

Arnold, David W. Recent Legislative Initiatives and Reactions by the Psychological Community. *The Industrial-Organizational Psychologist*, Volume 29, Number 2 (October 1991), pp. 29–31.

Arnold, David W. Potential Legislative Inroads into Personnel Psychology: Appropriate Reaction Measures. *Journal of Business and Psychology*, Volume 6, Number 2 (Winter 1991), pp. 279–282.

Arnold, David W. and Rachel A. Ankeny. A Review of 1992 State Anti-Testing Initiatives. *The Industrial-Organizational Psychologist*, Volume 30, Number 2 (October 1992), pp. 58–60.

Arnold, David W., John W. Jones, and William G. Harris. Evaluating the Integrity Test. *Security Management*, Volume 34, Number 4 (April 1990), pp. 63–66.

Arnold, David W. and Alan J. Thiemann. To Test or Not to Test: The Status of Psychological Testing under the Americans with Disabilities Act (ADA). *Journal of Business and Psychology*, Volume 6, Number 4 (Summer 1992), pp. 503–506.

Arvey, Richard D. and Paul R. Sackett. Fairness in Selection: Current Developments and Perspectives. In Neal Schmitt and Walter C. Borman (Eds.), *Personnel Selection in Organizations.* San Francisco: Jossey-Bass Publishers, 1993, pp. 171–202.

Ash, Philip. Screening Employment Applicants for Attitudes toward Theft. *Journal of Applied Psychology*, Volume 55, Number 2 (April 1971), pp. 161–164.

Ash, Philip. A History of Honesty Testing. In John W. Jones (Ed.), *Preemployment Honesty Testing*. Westport, Conn.: Quorum Books, 1991a, pp. 3–19.

Ash, Philip. Law and Regulation of Preemployment Inquiries. *Journal of Business and Psychology*, Volume 5, Number 3 (Spring 1991b), pp. 291–308.

Ash, Philip. Comparison of Two Integrity Tests Based upon Youthful or Adult Attitudes and Experiences. *Journal of Business and Psychology*, Volume 5, Number 3 (Spring 1991c), pp. 367–381.

Ash, Philip and Samuel J. Maurice. Rediscovering the First Clear Purpose Honesty Test. *Journal of Business and Psychology*, Volume 2, Number 4 (Summer 1988), pp. 378–382.

Association of Personnel Test Publishers. Task Force on Integrity Testing Practices. *Model Guidelines for Preemployment Integrity Testing Programs*. Washington, D.C.: The Association, 1991.

Barlow, Wayne E. Act to Accommodate the Disabled. *Personnel Journal*, Volume 10, Number 11 (November 1991), pp. 119–124.

Barlow, Wayne E. and Edward Z. Hane. A Practical Guide to the Americans with Disabilities Act. *Personnel Journal*, Volume 71, Number 6 (June 1992), pp. 53–60.

Barrick, Murray R. and Michael K. Mount. The Big Five Personality Dimensions and Job Performance: A Meta-Analysis. *Personnel Psychology*, Volume 44, Number 1 (Spring 1991), pp. 1–26.

Bashore, Theodore R. and Paul E. Rapp. Are There Alternatives to Traditional Polygraph Procedures? *Psychological Bulletin*, Volume 113, Number 1 (January 1993), pp. 3–22.

Baydoun, Ramzi B. and George A. Neuman. The Future of the General Aptitude Test Battery (GATB) for Use in Public and Private Testing. *Journal of Business and Psychology*, Volume 7, Number 1 (Fall 1992), pp. 81–91.

Ben-Shakhar, Gershon and Maya Bar-Hillel. Misconceptions in Martin and Terris's (1991) "Predicting Infrequent Behavior: Clarifying the Impact on False-Positive Rates." *Journal of Applied Psychology*, Volume 78, Number 1 (February 1993), pp. 148–150.

Ben-Shakhar, Gershon, Maya Bar-Hillel, Yoram Bilu, Edor Ben-Abba, and Anat Flug. Can Graphology Predict Occupational Success? Two Empirical Studies and Some Methodological Ramifications. *Journal of Applied Psychology*, Volume 71, Number 4 (November 1986), pp. 645–653.

Berman, Jeffrey A. Validation of the P.D.I. Employment Inventory in a Retail Chain. *Journal of Business and Psychology*, Volume 7, Number 4 (Summer 1993), pp. 413–419.

Bernardin, H. John and Donna K. Cooke. Validity of an Honesty Test in Predicting Theft among Convenience Store Employees. *Academy of Management Journal*, Volume 36, Number 5 (October 1993), pp. 1097–1108.

Biddle, Richard E. How to Set Cutoff Scores for Knowledge Tests Used in Promotion, Training, Certification, and Licensing. *Public Personnel Management*, Volume 22, Number 1 (Spring 1993), pp. 63–79.

Boye, Michael W. and Karen B. Slora. The Severity and Prevalence of Deviant Employee Activity within Supermarkets. *Journal of Business and Psychology*, Volume 8, Number 2 (Winter 1993), pp. 245–253.

Brown, Dianne C. EEOC Rules on the Americans with Disabilities Act: Will We Still

Be Testing? *The Industrial-Organizational Psychologist*, Volume 29, Number 3 (January 1992), pp. 50–51.

Camara, Wayne J. OTA Releases Report on Integrity Testing. *The Industrial-Organizational Psychologist*. Volume 28, Number 3 (January 1991), pp. 49–50.

Camara, Wayne J. and Dianne L. Schneider. Integrity Tests: Facts and Unresolved Issues. *American Psychologist*, Volume 49, Number 2 (February 1994), pp. 112–119.

Capps, Michael H. Can We Still Pick Out the Bad Apples? *Security Management*, Volume 33, Number 10 (October 1989), pp. 126, 128.

Capps, Michael H. Accuracy of Individual Parameters in Field Polygraph Studies. *Polygraph*, Volume 20, Number 2 (1991), pp. 65–69.

Capps, Michael H. and Norman Ansley. Analysis of Federal Polygraph Charts by Spot and Chart Total. *Polygraph*, Volume 21, Number 2 (1992), pp. 110–131.

Capps, Michael H., Brenda L. Knill, Ronnie K. Evans, and G. J. Johnson. Cognitive Arousal as a Means of Evaluation. *Polygraph*, Volume 24, Number 1 (1995), pp. 1–5.

Cascio, Wayne F., Ralph A. Alexander, and Gerald V. Barrett. Setting Cutoff Scores: Legal, Psychometric, and Professional Issues and Guidelines. *Personnel Psychology*, Volume 41, Number 1 (Spring 1988), pp. 1–24.

Chen, Peter Y. and Paul E. Spector. Relationships of Work Stressors with Aggression, Withdrawal, Theft and Substance Use: An Exploratory Study. *Journal of Occupational and Organizational Psychology*, Volume 65, Number 3 (September 1992), pp. 177–184.

Collins, Judith M. and Frank L. Schmidt. Personality, Integrity, and White Collar Crime: A Construct Validity Study. *Personnel Psychology*, Volume 46, Number 2 (Summer 1993), pp. 295–311.

Cook, John C. Preparing for Statistical Battles under the Civil Rights Act. *HR Focus*, Volume 69, Number 5 (May 1992), pp. 12–13.

Cortina, Jose M. What is Coefficient Alpha? An Examination of Theory and Applications. *Journal of Applied Psychology*, Volume 78, Number 1 (February 1993), pp. 98–104.

Crino, Michael D. and Terry L. Leap. What HR Managers Must Know about Employee Sabotage. *Personnel*, Volume 66, Number 5 (May 1989), pp. 31–38.

Cropanzano, Russell and Mary Konovsky. Drug Use and Its Implications for Employee Drug Testing. *Research in Personnel and Human Resource Management*, Volume 11 (1993), pp. 207–257.

Cunningham, Michael R. Test-taking Motivations and Outcomes on a Standardized Measure of On-the-job Integrity. *Journal of Business and Psychology*, Volume 4, Number 1 (Fall 1989), pp. 119–127.

Cunningham, Michael R. and Philip Ash. The Structure of Honesty: Factor Analysis of the Reid Report. *Journal of Business and Psychology*, Volume 3, Number 1 (Fall 1988), pp. 54–66.

Cunningham, Michael R., Dennis T. Wong, and Anita P. Barbee. Self-presentation Dynamics on Overt Integrity Tests: Experimental Studies of the Reid Report. *Journal of Applied Psychology*, Volume 79, Number 5 (October 1994), pp. 643–658.

Dalton, Dan R., Michael B. Metzger, and James C. Wimbush. Integrity Testing for Personnel Selection: A Review and Research Agenda. *Research in Personnel and Human Resources Management*, Volume 12 (1994), pp. 125–160.

Dean, Carol C., Charles D. Ramser, and Al B. Krienke. The Technology of Personnel

Selection: The Effect of Applicants' Faking on Honesty Test Vendors' Assessments. *Southern Management Association Proceedings*, 1995.

DeAngelis, Tori. Honesty Tests Weigh in with Improved Ratings. *APA Monitor*, June 1991, p. 7.

Dipboye, Robert L. *Selection Interviews: Process Perspectives*. Cincinnati: South-Western Publishing Company, 1992.

Eagly, Alice H. and Blair T. Johnson. Gender and Leadership Style: A Meta-analysis. *Psychological Bulletin*, Volume 108, Number 2 (September 1990), pp. 233–256.

Ekman, Paul and Maureen O'Sullivan. Who Can Catch a Liar? *American Psychologist*, Volume 46, Number 9 (September 1991), pp. 913–920.

Elliott, Robert H. and Deborah T. Jarrett. Violence in the Workplace: The Role of Human Resource Management. *Public Personnel Management*, Volume 23, Number 2 (Summer 1994), pp. 287–299.

Equal Employment Opportunity Commission (EEOC). *Enforcement Guidance on Pre-employment Disability-Related Inquiries and Medical Examinations under the Americans with Disabilities Act of 1990*. Washington, D.C.: U.S. Government Printing Office, 1994.

Frost, Alan G. and Joseph A. Orban. An Examination of an Appropriateness Index and Its Effect on Validity Coefficients. *Journal of Business and Psychology*, Volume 5, Number 1 (Fall 1990), pp. 23–36.

Frost, Alan G. and Fred M. Rafilson. Overt Integrity Tests versus Personality-Based Measures of Delinquency: An Empirical Comparison. *Journal of Business and Psychology*, Volume 3, Number 3 (Spring 1989), pp. 269–277.

Giacalone, Robert A. and Paul Rosenfeld. Reasons for Employee Sabotage in the Workplace. *Journal of Business and Psychology*, Volume 1, Number 4 (Summer 1987), pp. 367–378.

Ghiselli, Edwin E. *Explorations in Managerial Talent*. Pacific Palisades, Calif.: Goodyear Publishing Company, 1971.

Gleason, Philip M., Jonathan R. Veum, and Michael R. Pergamit. Drug and Alcohol Use at Work: A Survey of Young Workers. *Monthly Labor Review*, Volume 114, Number 8 (August 1991), pp. 3–7.

Goldberg, Lewis R., Julia R. Grenier, Robert M. Guion, Lee B. Sechrest, and Hilda Wing. *Questionnaires Used in the Prediction of Trustworthiness in Pre-Employment Selection Decisions: An A.P.A. Task Force Report*. American Psychological Association, Science Directorate, 1991.

Gomes, Glenn M. and James F. Morgan. Meeting the Wrongful Discharge Challenge: Legislative Options for Small Business. *Journal of Small Business Management*, Volume 30, Number 4 (October 1992), pp. 96–105.

Gough, Harrison G. The Assessment of Wayward Impulse by Means of the Personnel Reaction Blank. *Personnel Psychology*, Volume 24, Number 4 (Winter 1971), pp. 669–677.

Greenberg, Jerald. Employee Theft as a Reaction to Underpayment Inequity: The Hidden Cost of Pay Cuts. *Journal of Applied Psychology*, Volume 75, Number 5 (October 1990), pp. 561–568.

Greenberg, Jerald. Stealing in the Name of Justice: Informational and Interpersonal Moderators of Theft Reactions to Underpayment Inequity. *Organizational Behavior and Human Decision Processes*, Volume 54, Number 1 (February 1993), pp. 81–103.

Griggs v. Duke Power Company (1971), 401 U.S. 424.

Guastello, Stephen J. New Polygraph Law: No Dangerous Weaponry Involved. *The In-dustrial-Organizational Psychologist*, Volume 26, Number 3 (May 1989), pp. 48–50.

Guastello, Stephen J. and Mark L. Rieke. A Review and Critique of Honesty Test Research. *Behavioral Sciences and the Law*, Volume 9 (1991), pp. 501–523.

Guion, Robert M. *Personnel Testing*. New York: McGraw-Hill Book Company, 1965.

Haney, Walter M., George F. Madaus, and Robert Lyons. *The Fractured Marketplace for Standardized Testing*. Norwell, Mass.: Kluwer Academic Publishers, 1993.

Hanson, G. A. To Catch a Thief: The Legal and Policy Implications of Honesty Testing in the Workplace. *Law and Inequality*, Volume 9 (1991), pp. 497–531.

Harris, Michael M. and Laura L. Heft. Alcohol and Drug Use in the Workplace: Issues, Controversies, and Directions for Future Research. *Journal of Management*, Volume 18, Number 2 (June 1992), pp. 239–266.

Harris, Michael M. and Paul R. Sackett. A Factor Analysis and Item Response Theory Analysis of an Employee Honesty Test. *Journal of Business and Psychology*, Volume 2, Number 2 (Winter 1989), pp. 122–135.

Hartigan, John A. and Alexandra K. Wigdor. *Fairness in Employment Testing: Validity Generalization, Minority Issues, and the General Aptitude Test Battery*. Washington, D.C.: National Academy Press, 1989.

Harvey, Michael G. and Richard A. Cosier. Homicides in the Workplace: Crisis or False Alarm? *Business Horizons*, Volume 38, Number 2 (March-April 1995), pp. 11–20.

Heneman, Herbert G. and Robert L. Heneman. *Staffing Organizations*. Homewood, Ill.: Mendota House and Austen Press–Irwin, 1994.

Heshizer, Brian and Jan P. Muczyk. Drug Testing at the Workplace: Balancing Individual, Organizational, and Societal Rights. *Labor Law Journal*, Volume 39 (June 1988), pp. 342–357.

Hogan, Joyce and Robert Hogan. How to Measure Employee Reliability. *Journal of Applied Psychology*, Volume 74, Number 2 (April 1989), pp. 273–279.

Hollinger, Richard C. and John P. Clark. *Theft by Employees*. New York: Lexington Books, 1983.

Honts, Charles R., David C. Raskin, and John C. Kircher. Mental and Physical Countermeasures Reduce the Accuracy of Polygraph Tests. *Journal of Applied Psychology*, Volume 79, Number 2 (April 1994), pp. 252–259.

Hough, Leaetta M., Newell K. Eaton, Marvin D. Dunnette, John D. Kamp, and Rodney A. McCloy. Criterion-Related Validities of Personality Constructs and the Effect of Response Distortion on Those Validities. *Journal of Applied Psychology*, Volume 75, Number 5 (October 1990), pp. 581–595.

Hunsicker, J. Freedley. Ready or Not: The ADA. *Personnel Journal*, Volume 69, Number 8 (August 1990), pp. 81–83.

Inwald, Robin. How to Evaluate Psychological/Honesty Tests. *Personnel Journal*, Volume 67, Number 5 (May 1988), pp. 40–46.

Jones, Alan and Elizabeth Harrison. Prediction of Performance in Initial Officer Training Using Reference Reports. *Journal of Occupational Psychology*, Volume 55, Number 1 (March 1982), pp. 35–42.

Jones, John W. *Preemployment Honesty Testing: Current Research and Future Directions*. Westport, Conn.: Quorum Books, 1991a.

Jones, John W. Assessing Privacy Invasiveness of Psychological Test Items: Job Relevant versus Clinical Measures of Integrity. *Journal of Business and Psychology*, Volume 5, Number 4 (Summer 1991b), pp. 531–535.

Jones, John W., David Arnold, and William G. Harris. Introduction to the Model Guidelines for Preemployment Integrity Testing. *Journal of Business and Psychology*, Volume 4, Number 4 (Summer 1990), pp. 525–532.

Jones, John W., Philip Ash, Catalina Soto, and William Terris. Protecting Job Applicants' Privacy Rights When Using Preemployment Honesty Tests. In John W. Jones (Ed.), *Preemployment Honesty Testing*. Westport, Conn.: Quorum Books, 1991, pp. 229–238.

Jones, John W. and Joseph A. Orban. An Evaluation of a Brief Integrity Test User Orientation Program. *Journal of Business and Psychology*, Volume 7, Number 1 (Fall 1992), pp. 93–97.

Kamp, John and Paul Brooks. Perceived Organizational Climate and Employee Counterproductivity. *Journal of Business and Psychology*, Volume 5, Number 4 (Summer 1991), pp. 447–458.

Kinard, Jerry and Stanley Renas. Negligent Hiring: Are Hospitals Vulnerable? *Public Personnel Management*, Volume 20, Number 3 (Fall 1991), pp. 263–270.

Knatz, Hilary F., Robin E. Inwald, Albert L. Brockwell, and Linh N. Tran. IPI and MMPI Predictions of Counterproductive Job Behaviors by Racial Groups. *Journal of Business and Psychology*, Volume 7, Number 2 (Winter 1992), pp. 189–201.

Kobbs, Steven W. and Richard D. Arvey. Distinguishing Deviant and Non-Deviant Nurses Using the Personnel Reaction Blank. *Journal of Business and Psychology*, Volume 8, Number 2 (Winter 1993), pp. 255–264.

Kohl, John P. and Paul S. Greenlaw. The Americans with Disabilities Act of 1990: Implications for Managers. *Sloan Management Review*, Volume 33, Number 3 (Spring 1992), pp. 87–90.

Landy, Frank J., Laura J. Shankster, and Stacey S. Kohler. Personnel Selection and Placement. *Annual Review of Psychology*, Volume 45 (1994), pp. 261–296.

Langdon, Charles W. and William P. Galle. "... And What Was the Reason for Departure?" *Personnel Administrator*, Volume 34, Number 8 (August 1989), pp. 62–70.

Ledvinka, James and Vida G. Scarpello. *Federal Regulation of Personnel and Human Resource Management*. Boston: PWS–Kent Publishing, 1991.

Leo, John. The Color of the Law. *U.S. News and World Report*, Volume 119, Number 15 (October 16, 1995), p. 24.

Libbin, Anne, Susan R. Mendelsohn, and Dennis P. Duffy. The Right to Privacy at the Workplace, Part 5: Employee Medical and Honesty Testing. *Personnel*, Volume 65, Number 11 (November 1988), pp. 38–48.

Lilienfeld, Scott O., George Alliger, and Krystin Mitchell. Why Integrity Testing Remains Controversial. *American Psychologist*, Volume 50, Number 6 (June 1995), pp. 457–458.

LoBello, Steven G. and Benjamin N. Sims. Fakability of a Commercially Produced Pre-Employment Integrity Test. *Journal of Business and Psychology*, Volume 8, Number 2 (Winter 1993), pp. 265–273.

Lotito, Michael J. and Jamerson C. Allen. Answers to Commonly Asked ADA Questions. *Society for Human Resource Management Legal Report* (Summer 1992), pp. 1–8.

Manhardt, Philip J. Base Rates and Tests of Deception: Has I/O Psychology Shot Itself in the Foot? *The Industrial-Organizational Psychologist*, Volume 26, Number 2 (February 1989), pp. 48–50.

Mars, Gerald. *Cheats at Work: An Anthropology of Workplace Crime*. Brookfield, Vt.: Dartmouth Publishing Company, 1994.

Martin, Lynn. Drug-free Policy: Key to Success for Small Businesses. *HR Focus*, Volume 69, Number 9 (September 1992), p. 23.

Martin, Scott L. Honesty Testing: Estimating and Reducing the False Positive Rate. *Journal of Business and Psychology*, Volume 3, Number 3 (Spring 1989), pp. 255–267.

Martin, Scott L. Estimating the False Positive Rate for Alternative Measures of Integrity. *Journal of Business and Psychology*, Volume 4, Number 3 (Spring 1990), pp. 385–389.

Martin, Scott L. and Loren P. Lehnen. Select the Right Employees through Testing. *Personnel Journal*, Volume 71, Number 6 (June 1992), pp. 46–51.

Martin, Scott L. and William Terris. The Four-cell Classification Table in Personnel Selection: A Heuristic Device Gone Awry. *The Industrial-Organizational Psychologist*, Volume 27, Number 3 (May 1990), pp. 49–55.

Martin, Scott L. and William Terris. Predicting Infrequent Behavior: Clarifying the Impact on False-Positive Rates. *Journal of Applied Psychology*, Volume 76, Number 3 (June 1991), pp. 484–487.

McClelland, David C., John W. Atkinson, Russell A. Clark, and Edgar L. Lowell. *The Achievement Motive*. New York: Appleton-Century-Clark, Inc., 1953.

McClelland, David C. and David G. Winter. *Motivating Economic Achievement*. New York: The Free Press, 1969.

McDaniel, Michael A. Does Pre-employment Drug Use Predict On-the-job Suitability? *Personnel Psychology*, Volume 41, Number 4 (Winter 1988), pp. 717–729.

McDaniel, Michael A. Biographical Constructs for Predicting Employee Suitability. *Journal of Applied Psychology*, Volume 74, Number 6 (December 1989), pp. 964–970.

McDaniel, Michael A. and John W. Jones. A Meta-Analysis of the Validity of the Employee Attitude Inventory Theft Scales. *Journal of Business and Psychology*, Volume 1, Number 1 (Fall 1986), pp. 31–50.

McDaniel, Michael A. and John W. Jones. Predicting Employee Theft: A Quantitative Review of the Validity of a Standardized Measure of Dishonesty. *Journal of Business and Psychology*, Volume 2, Number 4 (Summer 1988), pp. 327–345.

Mental Measurements Yearbooks. The University of Nebraska Press and Buros Institute of Mental Measurements.

Miller, Edward J. Investing in a Drug-Free Workplace. *HR Magazine*, Volume 36, Number 5 (May 1991), pp. 48–51.

Miner, John B. *The Management Process: Theory, Research, and Practice*. New York: Macmillan Publishing Company, 1978.

Miner, John B. *Industrial-Organizational Psychology*. New York: McGraw-Hill Inc., 1992.

Miner, John B. *Role Motivation Theories*. New York: Routledge, 1993.

Miner, John B. and Michael H. Capps. Honesty Test Scores of Prison Inmates. *Polygraph*, Volume 19, Number 1 (1990), pp. 68–71.

Miner, John B. and Donald P. Crane. *Human Resource Management: The Strategic Perspective*. New York: HarperCollins Publishers, 1995.

Miner, John B., Bahman Ebrahimi, and Jeffrey M. Wachtel. How Deficiencies in Motivation to Manage Contribute to the United States' Competitiveness Problem (and What Can Be Done about It). *Human Resource Management*, Volume 34, Number 3 (Fall 1995), pp. 363–387.

Miner, John B., Norman R. Smith, and Jeffrey S. Bracker. Role of Entrepreneurial Task Motivation in the Growth of Technologically Innovative Firms: Interpretations from Follow-up Data. *Journal of Applied Psychology*, Volume 79, Number 4 (August 1994), pp. 627–630.

Moore, Robert W. Unmasking Thieves: From Polygraph to Paper. *Journal of Managerial Psychology*, Volume 3, Number 1 (1988), pp. 17–21.

Morrow, Ira J. Book review of *Preemployment Honesty Testing: Current Research and Future Directions*, by John W. Jones. *Personnel Psychology*, Volume 45, Number 3 (Autumn 1992), pp. 681–686.

Murphy, Kevin R. Detecting Infrequent Deception. *Journal of Applied Psychology*, Volume 72, Number 4 (November 1987), pp. 611–614.

Murphy, Kevin R. Maybe We *Should* Shoot Ourselves in the Foot: Reply to Manhardt. *The Industrial-Organizational Psychologist*, Volume 26, Number 3 (May 1989), pp. 45–46.

Murphy, Kevin R. *Honesty in the Workplace*. Pacific Grove, Calif.: Brooks/Cole Publishing Company, 1993.

Murphy, Kevin R. and Sandra L. Lee. Personality Variables Related to Integrity Test Scores: The Role of Conscientiousness. *Journal of Business and Psychology*, Volume 8, Number 4 (Summer 1994), pp. 413–424.

Nester, Mary Anne. *Implementing the Americans with Disabilities Act: Pre-Employment Testing and the ADA*. New York State School of Industrial and Labor Relations, Cornell University, 1994.

Normand, Jacques, Stephen D. Salyards, and John J. Mahoney. An Evaluation of Preemployment Drug Testing. *Journal of Applied Psychology*, Volume 75, Number 6 (December 1990), pp. 629–639.

O'Bannon, R. Michael, Linda A. Goldinger, and Gavin S. Appleby. *Honesty and Integrity Testing: A Practical Guide*. Atlanta: Applied Information Resources, 1989.

O'Meara, Daniel P. Personality Tests Raise Questions of Legality and Effectiveness. *HR Magazine*, Volume 39, Number 1 (January 1994), pp. 97–99.

Ones, Deniz S., Chockalingam Viswesvaran, and Frank L. Schmidt. Comprehensive Meta-Analysis of Integrity Test Validities: Findings and Implications for Personnel Selection and Theories of Job Performance. *Journal of Applied Psychology*, Volume 78, Number 4 (August 1993), pp. 679–703.

Ones, Deniz S., Chockalingam Viswesvaran, and Frank L. Schmidt. Integrity Tests: Overlooked Facts, Resolved Issues, and Remaining Questions. *American Psychologist*, Volume 50, Number 6 (June 1995), pp. 456–457.

Patrick, Christopher J. and William G. Iacono. Psychopathy, Threat, and Polygraph Test Accuracy. *Journal of Applied Psychology*, Volume 74, Number 2 (April 1989), pp. 347–355.

Paunonen, Sampo V., Douglas N. Jackson, and Steven M. Oberman. Personnel Selection Decisions: Effects of Applicant Personality and the Letter of Reference. *Organizational Behavior and Human Decision Processes*, Volume 40, Number 1 (August 1987), pp. 96–114.

Piotrowski, Zygmunt A. and Milton R. Rock. *The Perceptanalytic Executive Scale: A*

Tool for the Selection of Top Managers. New York: Grune & Stratton Inc., 1963.

Quirk, James H. HR Managers Face Legal Aspects of Workplace Violence. *HR Magazine*, Volume 38, Number 11 (November 1993), pp. 115–120.

Rafilson, Fred M. Development of a Standardized Measure to Predict Employee Productivity. *Journal of Business and Psychology*, Volume 3, Number 2 (Winter 1988), pp. 199–213.

Reynolds, Larry. ADA Complaints Are Not What Experts Predicted. *HR Focus*, Volume 70, Number 11 (November 1993), pp. 1, 6.

Reynolds, Larry. ADA Is Still Confusing after All These Years. *HR Focus*, Volume 71, Number 11 (November 1994), pp. 1, 8.

Rieke, Mark L. and Stephen J. Guastello. Unresolved Issues in Honesty and Integrity Testing. *American Psychologist*, Volume 50, Number 6 (June 1995), pp. 458–459.

Riley, M. J. A Paper and Pencil Test to Replace the Polygraph. *Central State Business Review*, Volume 1 (1982), p. 3.

Rosenbaum, Richard W. Predictability of Employee Theft Using Weighted Application Blanks. *Journal of Applied Psychology*, Volume 61, Number 1 (February 1976), pp. 94–98.

Rosenfeld, J. P. Alternative Views of Bashore and Rapp's (1993) Alternatives to Traditional Polygraphy: A Critique. *Psychological Bulletin*, Volume 117, Number 1 (January 1995), pp. 159–166.

Ryan, Ann M. and Marja Lasek. Negligent Hiring and Defamation: Areas of Liability Related to Pre-employment Inquiries. *Personnel Psychology*, Volume 44, Number 2 (Summer 1991), page 293–319.

Ryan, Ann M. and Paul R. Sackett. Pre-employment Honesty Testing: Fakability, Reactions of Test Takers, and Company Image. *Journal of Business and Psychology*, Volume 1, Number 3 (Spring 1987), pp. 248–256.

Rynes, Sara L. Who's Selecting Whom? Effects of Selection Practices on Applicant Attitudes and Behavior. In Neal Schmitt and Walter C. Borman (Eds.), *Personnel Selection in Organizations*. San Francisco: Jossey-Bass Publishers, 1993, pp. 240–274.

Rynes, Sara L. and Mary L. Connerley. Applicant Reactions to Alternative Selection Procedures. *Journal of Business and Psychology*, Volume 7, Number 3 (Spring 1993), pp. 261–277.

Sackett, Paul R. Integrity Testing for Personnel Selection. *Current Directions in Psychological Science*, Volume 3, Number 3 (June 1994), pp. 73–76.

Sackett, Paul R. and Phillip J. Decker. Detection of Deception in the Employment Context: A Review and Critical Analysis. *Personnel Psychology*, Volume 32, Number 3 (Autumn 1979), pp. 487–506.

Sackett, Paul R. and Michael M. Harris. Honesty Testing for Personnel Selection: A Review and Critique. *Personnel Psychology*, Volume 37, Number 2 (Summer 1984), pp. 221–245.

Sackett, Paul R. and Michael M. Harris. Honesty Testing for Personnel Selection: A Review and Critique. In H. John Bernardin and David A. Bownas (Eds.), *Personality Assessment in Organizations*. New York: Praeger Publishers, 1985, pp. 236–276. (This is an expanded version of the previous article.)

Sackett, Paul R., Laura R. Burris, and Christine Callahan. Integrity Testing for Personnel

Selection: An Update. *Personnel Psychology*, Volume 42, Number 3 (Autumn 1989), pp. 491–529.

Saxe, Leonard. Detection of Deception: Polygraph and Integrity Tests. *Current Directions in Psychological Science*, Volume 3, Number 3 (June 1994), pp. 69–73.

Schmidt, Frank L., Deniz S. Ones, and John E. Hunter. Personnel Selection. *Annual Review of Psychology*, Volume 43 (1992), pp. 627–670.

Schneider, Robert J. and Leaetta M. Hough. Personality and Industrial/Organizational Psychology. *International Review of Industrial and Organizational Psychology*, Volume 10 (1995), pp. 75–129.

Scientific Affairs Committee, Society for Industrial and Organizational Psychology. Use of Subgroup Norms in Employment-Related Tests: Technical Issues and Limitations. *The Industrial-Organizational Psychologist*, Volume 31, Number 2 (October 1993), pp. 44–49.

Segal, Jonathan A. Drugs, Alcohol and the ADA. *HR Magazine*, Volume 37, Number 12 (December 1992), pp. 73–76.

Seligman, Daniel. Searching for Integrity. *Fortune*, Volume 127, Number 5 (March 8, 1993), p. 140.

Slora, Karen B. An Empirical Approach to Determining Employee Deviance Base Rates. *Journal of Business and Psychology*, Volume 4, Number 2 (Winter 1989), pp. 199–219.

Smith, Patricia L. Personnel Rx for the Small-Business Owner. *HR Magazine*, Volume 36, Number 3 (March 1991), pp. 52–54.

Stone, Eugene F. and Diana L. Stone. Privacy in Organizations: Theoretical Issues, Research Findings, and Protection Mechanisms. *Research in Personnel and Human Resource Management*, Volume 8 (1990), pp. 349–411.

Stone, Romuald A. Workplace Homicide: A Time for Action. *Business Horizons*, Volume 38, November 2 (March-April 1995), pp. 3–10.

Streufert, Siegfried, Rosanne M. Pogash, John Roache, Dennis Gingrich, Richard Landis, Walter Severs, Lisa Lonardi, and Anne Kantner. Effects of Alcohol Intoxication on Risk Taking, Strategy, and Error Rate in Visuomotor Performance. *Journal of Applied Psychology*, Volume 77, Number 4 (August 1992), pp. 515–524.

Tansky, Judith W. and Marjorie Armstrong-Stassen. Integrity Tests: A Comparison of Two "Overt" Tests. *Southern Management Association Proceedings*, 1995.

Terpstra, David E. and Elizabeth J. Rozell. The Relationship of Staffing Practices to Organizational Level Measures of Performance. *Personnel Psychology*, Volume 46, Number 1 (Spring 1993), pp. 27–48.

Touby, Laurel. In the Company of Thieves. *Journal of Business Strategy*, Volume 15, Number 3 (May-June 1994), pp. 24–35.

Twomey, David P. *Equal Employment Opportunity Law*. Cincinnati: South-Western Publishing Company, 1994.

U.S. Congress, Office of Technology Assessment. *The Use of Integrity Tests for Pre-Employment Screening*. U.S. Government Printing Office, 1990.

Waln, Robert F. and Ronald G. Downey. Voice Stress Analysis: Use of Telephone Recordings. *Journal of Business and Psychology*, Volume 1, Number 4 (Summer 1987), pp. 379–389.

Whyte, William H. *The Organization Man*. New York: Simon and Schuster, Inc., 1956.

Wigdor, Alexandra K. and Paul R. Sackett. Employment Testing and Public Policy: The Case of the General Aptitude Test Battery. In Heinz Schuler, James L. Farr, and

Mike Smith (Eds.), *Personnel Selection and Assessment: Individual and Organizational Perspectives*. Hillsdale, N.J.: Lawrence Erlbaum Associates, Publishers,
1993, pp. 183–204.

Wise, Lois R. and Steven J. Charvat. Polygraph Testing in the Public Sector: The Status
of State Legislation. *Public Personnel Management*, Volume 19, Number 4 (Winter 1990), pp. 381–390.

Name Index

Subject Index

About the Authors

JOHN B. MINER currently has a professional practice in Eugene, Oregon, specializing in industrial psychology, human resource management, and entrepreneurship. He has an undergraduate degree in psychology from Princeton University, a master's degree in clinical psychology from Clark University, and a Ph.D. in personality theory and clinical psychology from Princeton. After holding research positions as a psychologist at Columbia University and The Atlantic Refining Company, he served on the faculties of the University of Oregon, the University of Maryland, Georgia State University, and the State University of New York (SUNY) at Buffalo. At SUNY he held the Donald S. Carmichael chair in human resources, was director of the Center for Entrepreneurial Leadership, and chaired his department. He has been awarded the honor of Fellow status by five professional organizations, has been Editor of the *Academy of Management Journal*, and was President of the Academy of Management. His prior publications include 37 books and monographs, well over 100 articles and book chapters, and several psychological tests.

MICHAEL H. CAPPS is Director of the Department of Defense Polygraph Institute, where he is responsible for the training of all federal examiners in forensic psychophysiology, has oversight of all research within the Defense Department related to detection of deception, and is the principal advisor to the Office of the Secretary of Defense on polygraph policy. He earned his B.S. in social science from Troy State University and his M.S. in applied psychology from the University of Baltimore. Previously he was a member of the executive council of Argenbright Holdings, Ltd. of Atlanta, Georgia, one of the nation's largest security companies, while holding positions as President of Argenbright Polygraph, Inc. and of a psychological testing subsidiary. Subsequently, after moving to the government, he directed the operation of Polygraph and Personnel Security Research, and then served as senior advisor for quality management to the Director of Security Research, National Security Agency, before taking his present position. He has served tenures as Executive Director and President of the American Polygraph Association, where he received the highest awards for research, writing, teaching, merit, and excellence. His publications include 12 articles in professional journals and other national publications.